Crucible is published quarterly by Hymns Ancient & Modern Ltd.
Registered Charity No. 270060

This publication is in collaboration with the Church of England's Division of Mission and Public Affairs; the William Temple Foundation.

Editorial board

Stephen Platten, Edward Cardale, Kate Pearson, Elaine Graham, Malcolm Brown, Chris Swift, Carol Wardman, Matt Bullimore, James Woodward, Peter Scott, Andrew Hayes (Reviews Editor) and Anna Lawrence (Managing Editor).

Correspondence and articles

Correspondence and articles for submission should be sent to Anna Lawrence at Hymns Ancient and Modern, anna@hymnsam.co.uk. Articles should be of about 3,000 words.
Books for review to should be sent to Dr Andrew Hayes, The Queen's Foundation, Somerset Road, Birmingham, B15 2QH.

Subscriptions

(for four copies): individual rate £20; institutions £27; international (includes airmail) £38. Single copies cost £6.
All prices included postage and packing. Cheques should be made payable to Crucible, and sent to: Crucible subscriptions, Subscription Manager, 13a Hellesdon Park Road, Norwich NR6 5DR.

Tel: 01603 785 910   Fax: 01603 624483.
crucible@hymnsam.co.uk

Direct Debit forms available from the same address

ISSN 0011-2100
ISBN 978-0-334-05961-5

Contents

Editorial

Health and Human Flourishing   3
Gillian Straine

Articles

She Has a Voice: How Encountering Christ   5
Should Break the Silence
Sarah Mullally

Public Health in Theological Context   17
Jim McManus

'Moral Injury' From Military Experience   30
Stephen Radley

Why Mother Church Should Care About   42
Her Children's Bodies
Jacqueline R Cameron

Forum

Home Truths: A Theological Reflection   54
on Social Housing
Mike Long

Book Reviews

James Woodward, David Mark Dunning,   62
Charity Hamilton, Jayme R. Reaves, Stephen Platten

Editorial

Health and Human Flourishing

GILLIAN STRAINE

I am very grateful for the opportunity to edit this Health and Human Flourishing issue of Crucible, and I am indebted to the four authors who found time to write about health from their own unique perspectives.

From an ethical point of view, health is a topic which is almost limitless in its scope, especially from a faith perspective. In this field there has often been an obsession with definitions and boundaries. Indeed, in going through the archives of the charity I run, it's clear that each generation of Christians have asked, 'What is Health?', 'What is Healing?' and 'How and why does God act when we pray?'. Such questions are vital, but not the focus here.

Instead, you will find an expansive selection of articles with a focus on action, all written by Christians working in a complex health landscape to answer urgent questions of our day.

One of the problems in bringing together faith and health is a lack of confidence to engage in a field dominated by professionalism and science. But I would argue that our communities need Christians with a holistic understanding of human beings, in order to promote the type of flourishing that God can bring to people and communities buckling under multifaceted suffering and isolation.

The medicalisation and clinicalisation of twenty first century health has led to the domination of the healing of the individual body, with scant consideration of the search for what it is to be fully human. Despite the historical encounter of Christianity and public health, there is a need in contemporary times for a critical dialogue to reconcile understandings of health, illness and healing.

Bonhoeffer described health as 'the penultimate good' ; health is of

Editorial

course important and necessary for much of life, but for the Christian, it should be understood in its appropriate eschatological perspective. This standpoint adds an important corrective to an overly positivist or essentialist medical model and addresses the ethical issues of relating fully healthy to fully human. Both of these issues can be found in the WHO definition of health as, 'a state of complete physical, mental and social well-being and not merely the absence of disease or infirmity'. I find it a haunting statement.

Oxford theologian Nigel Biggar has recently argued that theological beliefs should be allowed a seat at the secularist political and social discussions regarding public policy. They should be able to express a credal affirmation of the special dignity of humans who, for many faiths, are made in the image of God. All four articles add here to this critical debate, presenting their version of God's desire that we flourish and bring flourishing to the communities we serve.

The Revd. Dr. Gillian Straine, The Guild of Health and St Raphael
www.gohealth.org.uk

Notes

1. Hashum Mahmood, *Collaborative Public Health and Christian Healing: A Critical Conversation, Master's Thesis*, University of Birmingham, Sept 2019.
2. Dietrich Bonhoeffer, *Ethics*, Minneapolis: Fortress, 2005.
3. Pattison, *Alive and Kicking: Towards a Practical theology of illness and healing*, SCM Press.
4. WHO, Preamble to the Constitution of World Health Organisation as adopted by the International Health Conference, 1948.
5. Nigel Bigger, 'Why religion deserves a place in secular medicine' *Journal of Medical Ethics*, Vol. 41, No. 3 p229-233.

She Has a Voice

How Encountering Christ Should Break the Silence

SARAH MULLALLY

The world wants to be well

We all want to feel good and positive about life. In recent history, both the academic world and popular culture have gravitated to the language of 'wellbeing' to begin to capture this (Linton, 1). The most basic definition of wellbeing is 'judging life positively and feeling good' (Cdc.gov, 2018). But what that takes to achieve is difficult to pin down. Western Society is far more used to a medical model. Our bodies are either at ease or diseased; functioning or malfunctioning. Within this model, illness is relatively easy to identify and pathways to repair pathology researched and put into place. Things are less straightforward when it comes to wellbeing. *Feeling good*, is clearly more subjective than *being ill*. And there is no consensus on what it means to be 'well' in this broader sense.

Despite the fact that understanding wellbeing is complex, a common thread running through the literature on wellness, is that we need to think more holistically about our lives. Our economic, social and emotional circumstances all play a part. This is not to say that identifying and treating illness is unimportant. If we get cancer, we want the quickest diagnosis and the best possible treatment. I have spent a significant proportion of my working life seeking to address such illness. However, understanding how to address this broader vision of wellness is also important. Researchers have found that a greater sense of wellbeing leads to greater physical and mental health, speedier recovery, greater productivity and greater levels of contribution to community (Cdc.gov, 2018).

The World Health Organisation's definition of health understands this need to address a broader definition of what it means to be well. It defines health as: 'a state of complete physical, mental and social well-being and not merely the absence of disease or infirmity' (Who.int, 2019). Likewise, Sir Michael Marmot and others have begun to highlight how crucial this kind of broad definition is to health.

This has always been obvious to nurses. The very nature of the profession is to seek to address more than the mere pathology. Nurses are aware of the needs of the whole person and are adept at providing care in such a way so as to empower the people they serve (see also Davies, 5). Florence Nightingale once said, 'A little needle work, a little writing, a little cleaning, would be the greatest relief the sick could have' (Karimi and Masoudi Alavi, 2015). In other words, we want to help people to be 'well' in every sense. However, there is no doubt that there has been a burgeoning quantity of research, literature and measurement of wellbeing in the last twenty years.

This increased interest in wellbeing isn't just the yearning of a particular culture, profession or historical moment. It is the direction of history. The story of the bible is one that ends in a profound sense of wellbeing. The term found in the scriptures for this is 'shalom' or 'peace'. It means more than just the absence of conflict. It means to live at peace with Christ, our community and his creation in such a way that our satisfaction, safety and sense of sufficiency flourishes in every way. The promise of shalom has always been God's message to exiles awaiting their promised land. This is what people need and want when they feel anxious or feel that their lives are hanging by a thread. It is a promise that one day things that hurt would lose out to things that heal and restore. Scripture speaks, for example, of physical shalom (Ps 4.8; Gen 43.27), relational shalom (1 Kings 5.12), and social and environmental shalom (Jer 29.5).

This similarity between the yearning of scripture and the yearning of culture means that, in some sense, the world recognises the need for what the Church offers - a journey towards shalom. As we offer encounter with God, we offer an invitation to journey with that God towards the peace that we all yearn for.

We see glimpses of shalom here in God's new community, the Church. It is meant to be, in the words of Stanley Haeurwas, 'A Peaceable Kingdom', where the Kingdom of God that we await from heaven, makes itself known in embryonic form here on earth (Hauerwas, 1984). We gather to worship the Prince of Peace, offer one another the sign of peace, and are sent out to seek peace. As we do so, we know something of the peace that transcends all understanding, guarding us and guiding us.

Despite this idyllic picture, anyone who is actually part of the Church will know that we have not arrived. We live in an 'in-between' time of the Kingdom of God - the now and not-yet. The Church's expression of shalom is imperfect. We see Christ imperfectly, do community deficiently and steward creation poorly. For example, as Walter Brueggemann says, when we share communion together, we not only tell a past but dream a future (De Beer, 9-10). A future in which shalom has finally come, and we feast at the marriage supper of the lamb (Rev 19).

It is into this picture of the now and not-yet, that I want to offer some thoughts on a distinctive Christian contribution to the conversation around wellbeing. I want to suggest one way in which encountering God moves us, albeit imperfectly, on a journey towards shalom.

My suggestion is this: encountering God is meant to restore our 'voice.' By voice, I mean a sense that what we have to say matters and that we are able to offer it meaningfully into our community. This is important because having a voice is tied up with a sense of being well. Because we live in this 'in between' time, the way that this is expressed in the life of the Church will be flawed, incomplete and require us to ask hard questions of ourselves. Nevertheless, I believe that the Church has a story to tell.

The importance of voice

It has been recently recognised that one aspect that contributes significantly to wellbeing is a sense of agency. Pritpal Tamber and Bridget Kelly, of the think tank Bridging Health & Community, recently published research that confirms what is widely accepted - that 'a sense of agency' is a powerful indicator of health (Tamber, 7). This can mean several things:

1. a belief that events can be determined by our behaviour (as opposed to fate);
2. a belief that we could act in a way that would produce a particular change;
3. that 'someone believes he or she is able to offer their opinion on,

or interpretation of, a situation or event' (Tamber, 39).

Implicit in 1 and 2 is the third definition and it is this that I particularly want to focus on. It suggests that creating a context in which people feel able to express their views, is a powerful component on the road to wellbeing. Rebecca Solnit wrote recently, referring to women in particular, that:

'Being unable to tell your story is a living death, and sometimes a literal one. If no one listens when you say your ex-husband is trying to kill you, if no one believes you when you say you are in pain, if no one hears you when you say help, if you don't dare say help, if you have been trained not to bother people by saying help. If you are considered to be out of line when you speak up in a meeting, are not admitted into an institution of power, are subject to irrelevant criticism whose subtext is that women should not be here or heard, [then you experience a kind of living death] … A free person tells her own story. A valued person lives in a society in which her story has a place' (Solnit, 2019). I want to explore how encounter with God is meant to give people a voice within the community of faith. If this is true, then two things need to be said. First, this is a distinctive area in which faith can contribute to our wellbeing. Secondly though, as we live in the 'now and not yet' of the Kingdom of God, we will observe that we still have a long way to go in order to make this, a more pervasive reality.

How Christ breaks the silence

I want to focus on one account in the ministry of Jesus that illustrates how encountering God gives us a voice. It is the events surrounding the bleeding woman recorded in Mark 5.24–34 and Luke 8.40–56.

The story will be a familiar one: Jesus is implored by an eminent local dignitary to accompany him to his house to heal his daughter. Jesus agrees but his journey is interrupted by the touch of a woman who has been bleeding for twelve years. All attempts by the healthcare system of the day have failed. She appears on the scene as a penniless outcast. In the end, both she and Jairus' daughter are healed. However, the details of the encounter reveal much more about how encountering Jesus changes us.

At the beginning of the story the woman has no name (we are not told her identity) and no voice (she is ceremonially unclean and so outside of the town / community). There is no easy access to people even if she wanted to speak.

Encountering Jesus changes the way that the woman uses her voice. He empowers the woman to speak. He will not simply let her go without her revealing herself and publicly expressing her faith. In this way Jesus enables her to use her voice once more among those she may have been alienated from. Although we don't find out her actual name, she is given privileged status by being addressed as 'daughter', which adds to the sense of her welcome back into the community.

It seems therefore as if, part of Jesus' ministry is to enhance our voices. He encourages the woman to own her voice. She was always a 'daughter' but needed encouragement to see it. Her faith in Christ enables her voice to be heard.

Jesus doesn't merely speak *on behalf* of the bleeding woman. This is more than merely speaking up *on behalf* of those who cannot speak for themselves (Prov 31.8). Jesus is creating an environment where someone who has been unable to speak can speak in her own words - sing her own song.

This is not the only thing going on in this miracle. It is not just *that* she speaks but *what* she speaks that is also in view. Nevertheless, in terms of my focus here, the significant point is that rather than merely *speak for* this woman, Jesus empowers her to *speak for herself*.

This picture is not unique to this miracle. Lepers are able to 'talk freely' (Mk 1.45), the man in the country of the Gerasenes is no longer isolated and controlled but can 'declare how much God has done' (Lk 8.26-29, 39). Bartimaeus was told by the crowd outside Jericho to 'be silent' and yet Jesus both encourages him to speak before the crowd and sends him away glorifying God (Lk 18.35-43). Jesus creates the space for those who have been unable to speak to sing their own song. A song that inevitably ends up bringing glory to Him.

Songs out of the silence

What we have been encountering in the scriptures is that as people interact with the hope that Christ offers and are welcomed into his community, they gain a voice. So now we can connect what we observed about a sense of agency with this observation about hope in Christ. Agency (or we could say 'voice') seems to positively influence wellbeing. So, it should not surprise us that where people are being enabled to use their voice in Christian communities today, we see significant gains in wellbeing. In this section I want to unpack some examples of where we have seen this in operation in my current context in the Diocese of London.

People who are disabled
Wave (which stands for 'We Are all Valued Equally') is a charity based in Muswell Hill Methodist Church that brings together those with and without disabilities for a range of activities week by week. It was established by parents whose Christian faith motivated them to work toward overcoming barriers to inclusion and social isolation, particularly with respect to disability. Jess is one beneficiary. She loves writing poetry, but it is only recently, through Wave, that she has started to perform it. The poems give real insight into how she sees the world around her, and also how she feels about it as she signs them in Makaton. She says that performing alongside others helps her to feel that 'everything's going to be OK' (Wave-for-change.org.uk, 2016). Jess' story demonstrates how encountering Christ and his community has given her a voice. A voice that has given her confidence and a sense of hope.

People who are elderly
Another example within the Diocese of London is the work of the 'Posh Club' run by St Paul's West Hackney. It's a weekly cabaret-style party for the over 60s that combats isolation and loneliness in the community. This provides a unique way to experience connection, laughter and physical activity while also being part of something that's vibrant and exciting. Father Niall Weir, Rector of St Paul's, says: 'If there was a Posh Club in every town in the UK, I'm certain the numbers of elderly on GP waiting lists would go down hugely'. Father Niall's reflection is that as the Christian community has given local residents an opportunity to be heard, reducing the burden on healthcare services.

People who are refugees
In 2016, St Paul's Cathedral was privileged to host the, 'I am a Refugee' campaign developed by The Joint Council for the Welfare of Immigrants (JCWI). Tricia Hillas, Canon Pastor at St Paul's, said that it invited us, 'to listen to the stories and celebrate the achievements of those who have entered the UK as refugees; our friends and neighbours, brothers and sisters who, through their unique contributions in a wide range of spheres, enhance our society and our lives'. In a time when many

refugees have sensed an atmosphere of hostility, victimisation and racism, the Christian community is seeking to allow stories to be shared and voices to be heard (Acik, 2015).

Enabling others to sing

These are wonderful stories of how people have been enabled to 'sing.' To use their voices where previously shame or structural barriers prevented them from doing so before.

It would, however, be wrong to think that there is room for triumphalism at this point. We live in the 'now and not yet' of the Church age and in the midst of a broken world. The initiatives that I have mentioned exist because something has been missing in those communities and, more than that, in the church. A few dedicated individuals have had a desire for change and the resolve to spearhead it.

For example, the reason that the Wave project was set up was because its founders felt the pain of seeing their children left out and on the edge of their community in Muswell Hill. They did not have a voice. They had felt first-hand the vulnerability of feeling like a burden rather than a source of blessing to those around them.

The Rector at St Paul's Haringey, Niall Weir, has said: 'There is a serious issue lying behind The Posh Club, which is loneliness and isolation in our communities'. Many in West Hackney did not have a voice.

One of the sad consequences of the Brexit campaign was the increased suspicion and hate crime aimed at refugees (James, 2016). Despite campaigns like the one at St Paul's, the voices of refugees has not always been welcome.

In addition, these initiatives reach a limited number of people in a limited number of geographical areas. Given the scale of disenfranchisement in our society and even in the church, they are just a drop in the ocean.

Undoubtedly though, the starkest failure of the Church to listen is in the area of safeguarding. Historically, there have been incidents where victims of abuse have been ignored. They did not have a voice. It horrifies me that people in positions of trust have abused individuals and that the Church has been slow to respond. When the Christ we worship demands that those on the margins are included and their voices amplified, we have too often be content to nurture the very opposite response.

To summarise at this point, my argument has been that:

1. Part of what it means to be well is to be able to be listened to and have a sense that what you say is taken seriously. Terms like 'agency' or 'voice' might be used to describe this;
2. In a number of the healing miracles of Jesus, he seems interested in doing more than merely healing a particular physical ailment, but also enabling the voices of those he interacts with to be heard;
3. As we the church, share the hope of Christ and interact with our communities, we have an opportunity to 'restore their voices' and so encourage their wellbeing;
4. In our local contexts, Christians can point to examples of where this is already happening;
5. This restoration of voices in the church, however, will always be imperfect. Both our hearts and our environments remain affected by sin.

In light of this, what impact might the Church have on the wider conversation around wellbeing?

The voice of Christ begins the process

We must continue to share the message of the gospel, our Christian hope. I know of many stories of where those who have embraced faith in Christ have been able to move beyond shame and a deep sense of guilt to speak of their experience and contribute to the life of the Church with great confidence. This has significantly improved their sense of wellbeing.

The voices in the Church can continue the process

In the case of the woman in Luke 8, Jesus had to actively encourage her to live that out as well. This job now falls, in part, to the church. Church communities should encourage those who have felt overlooked and undervalued to be able to speak and have their voices heard.

One example from my own diocese would be the work that the diocese are embarking on with female and BAME clergy. We want to dedicate more time and space as senior staff to listen carefully to their concerns, hopes and fears.

The voice of the national Church can champion this process

The national Church has a role in championing the voices of those who might not otherwise be heard.

I mentioned the mistakes of the past with respect to safeguarding. New training aims to ensure that there is a clearer process around how disclosures of abuse are heard and survivors' voices are enabled to improve things further.

The prophetic voice of the Church can promote it

Finally, the Church has the privileged role of challenging the government by speaking up for those whose voices might not be heard. One obvious area related to wellbeing is the current healthcare system. As I have repeatedly emphasised, there is no room for triumphalism at this point. We advocate for others from a place of repentant humility rather than a sense of successful confidence.

However, if voice is a significant factor in our wellbeing, then there are some very practical suggestions that we could make to move further in this direction.

> 1. Ensuring that when care is being organised or reviewed in a particular region, the local community is asked what wellbeing looks like for them and are given the opportunity to voice how to achieve it. This might look like setting up learning communities where policy makers and participants both have seats at the table. Notably, Tamber and Kelly point out that, 'A sense of being able to come together to create change is conceivably as core to the health of a community as a sense of control is to an individual's health' (Tamber, 7).

> 2. Listening more carefully to the voices of healthcare professionals. Dr Caroline Elton, an occupational psychologist, recently quoted the feelings of one of the GP's who visited her, only 6 years after completing her training. She said: '[The NHS] just doesn't care. It chews people up, spits them out, and then gets another well meaning chump to replace them' (Elton, 2019). Just as the Church needs to ensure that we care adequately for the wellbeing of our clergy, so the NHS needs to listen to and care for its staff.

Conclusion

Being well is something much more complex than not being ill, something which, even in secular literature, begins to look like the bible's picture of shalom. This is the Christian hope: a holistic peace that involves everything from how near we feel to others, to our neighbourhoods and crucially an ability to contribute meaningfully to them.

Being able to contribute to our communities, or being able to 'find our voice', begins in the present for those who encounter Christ and his community, and can genuinely contribute to our sense of wellbeing.

It is true that the story of the Church in this area is not a wholly positive one. It is a story littered with failure and a road on which we have much further to travel. Moving in the direction of empowering voices will involve time, whole communities and a person-centred approach. It will not necessarily be easy to organise or implement. It will meet with resistance. Yet as we live out our call to imitate our Saviour, we must take this challenge seriously. Perhaps it is an opportunity to not only display Christian love, but to offer a unique means of healing that is often missed.

The Right Reverend and Right Honourable Dame Sarah Mullally is Bishop of London
Bishop Sarah was formerly the UK's Chief Nursing Officer and the National Health Service's director of patient experience for England

Discussion Questions:

1. Have you observed the benefit of empowering people in your community to have a voice?
2. Who could benefit from being encouraged to have a voice in your community?
3. What might the next step look like to make this happen?

References

Acik, N. (2015). *Experiences of Young Migrant Men and Their Well-Being*. [online] Hummedia.manchester.ac.uk. Available at: http://hummedia.manchester.ac.uk/schools/law/main/cccj/mimen_final_synthesis_report%20_dec_15-v1.pdf [Accessed 3 Jun. 2019].

Cdc.gov. (2018). *Well-Being Concepts | HRQOL | CDC*. [online] Available at: https://www.cdc.gov/hrqol/wellbeing.htm [Accessed 3 June. 2019].

Davies, N., 2016, *The value and contribution of nursing to public health in the UK*, London: Royal College of Nursing.

Davies, M. (2018). *'God asked me to change this'*. [online] Churchtimes.co.uk. Available at: https://www.churchtimes.co.uk/articles/2018/9-march/news/uk/god-asked-me-to-change-this [Accessed 3 Jun. 2019].

De Beer, S.F., 2014, 'Demythologising social cohesion: Towards a practical theological vision', *Verbum et Ecclesia* 35(2), Art. #1344, 12 pages. Available at: http://dx.doi.org/10.4102/ve.v35i2.134 [Accessed 3 Jun. 2019].

Diocese of London. (2017). *Start a Conversation: lead the way on tackling isolation*. [online] Available at: https://www.london.anglican.org/articles/start-conversation-lead-way-tackling-isolation/ [Accessed 3 Jun. 2019].

Elton, C. (2019). *Doctors can't care for patients if the system doesn't care for them*. [online] bmj.com. Available at: https://www.bmj.com/content/364/bmj.l968 [Accessed 3 Jun. 2019].

James, C. (2016). *What are the consequences of Brexit for the refugee crisis?*. [online] Newstatesman.com. Available at: https://www.newstatesman.com/politics/uk/2016/06/what-are-consequences-brexit-refugee-crisis [Accessed 3 Jun. 2019].

Karimi, H. and Masoudi Alavi, N. (2015). *Florence Nightingale: The Mother of Nursing*. [online] Nursing and Midwifery Studies. Available at: https://www.ncbi.nlm.nih.gov/pmc/articles/PMC4557413/ [Accessed 3 Jun. 2019].

Hauerwas, S. (1984). *The Peaceable Kingdom: A Primer in Christian Ethics*, Michigan: University of Notre Dame Press.

Linton, M. (2019). *Review of 99 self-report measures for assessing wellbeing in adults: exploring dimensions of well-being and developments over time*. [online] bmj.com. Available at: https://bmjopen.bmj.com/content/bmjopen/6/7/e010641.full.pdf [Accessed 3 June. 2019].

Solnit, R. (2019). *Silence and powerlessness go hand in hand – women's voices must be heard* | Rebecca Solnit. [online] *The Guardian*. Available at: https://www.theguardian.com/commentisfree/2017/mar/08/silence-powerlessness-womens-voices-rebecca-solnit [Accessed 8 Mar. 2017].

Tamber, P. and Kelly, B. (2017). *Fostering Agency to Improve Health*. [online] Available at: https://www.pstamber.com/reports/register-to-download-the-full-report-fostering-agency-to-improve-health/ [Accessed 3 Jun. 2019]

Who.int. (2019). *Constitution*. [online] Available at: https://www.who.int/about/who-we-are/constitution [Accessed 3 Jun. 2019].

Public Health in Theological Context

Jim McManus

The reductionist biomedical model of health (biological dysfunction and disease needs to be cured) is increasingly problematic and fails to explain the multi-dimensional nature of the human person, or so we've been saying for forty years. It undoubtedly has value. When I had cancer, I needed that model to do its work to treat me. But it is not an unproblematic way of conceptualising health. As a public health practitioner it remains a too dominant discourse. As a result it is perennially difficult for the well evidenced insights that our social, economic, environmental and interpersonal circumstances shape our health far more than our biology to get traction in public policy

Any reading of the scientific literature on the social and economic determinants of health demonstrates that a range of factors including access to education, access to meaningful and fair work, housing and a sustainable environment free from pollution are foundational for good health status. Inability to enjoy these basic goods results in poorer health and earlier death (Marmot et al, 1661). Those with better education and better employment tend to access health services more effectively, and have better services than the poor.

Health is a key economic asset to states and communities. While genetics and behaviour play a part in our health outcomes (for example, length of life, predisposition to disease) the idea that health is entirely about individual behaviour is inaccurate. Healthy eating is not just about individual choice. Being able to afford it and being able to access shops with supplies of healthier choices are also important. "Food deserts" – areas where access to fresh and healthy food is worst – worsen health outcomes and are worst in areas of lowest income (Corfe, 2018.) The choices we can make are determined by our income, educational status, ability to understand what will improve and protect our health, and the ability to access and benefit from that. Health is social, or it is nothing. And the conditions to be healthy are social, not individual (Marmot, 2010).

To compound this, many health interventions driven by the individual biomedical model are aimed purely at individual behaviour patterns and tend to worsen inequalities in health because they privilege those better able to perform them – the well educated and well-paid. Similarly, health services aimed at everyone can increase inequalities because those who can access them best are those who are best off. This is famously called the Inverse Care Law. A social gradient in health outcomes and the means to achieve good health which privileges the privileged is at work. I cannot but conclude this is a theological, not just a scientific issue.

What do we mean by Health anyway?

When we use the word 'Health?' in varying contexts the term can be vague and all-encompassing. There is a significant and enduring interest in human health, across scientific and religious contexts (Fountain, 1999). There is no single consensus on what 'health' really means. The World Health Organisation (WHO) definition of health is a 'state of complete physical, mental and social well-being and not merely the absence of disease or infirmity' (World Health Organisation, 1946).

This feels tautological – 'health is a complete state of well-being'. Many scientific definitions of health remain concerned either with functional ability, absence of organic disease or a vague sense of wellbeing (Porter, 2010). It is difficult to argue against the WHO definition, precisely because it is so vague and all-encompassing.

If we simply assume the WHO definition uncritically, we consign a third of the population to never being truly healthy, by definition. The evidence of people living, they would say thriving and flourishing, with long term conditions, such as HIV, for many years (McManus, et al., 2012) shows that the WHO definition simply becomes difficult to apply to some populations who do not meet the definition but are thriving. (Slogrove, et al., 2018). How can one live well, with conditions which seem to contradict aspects of the WHO definition?

Epidemiology suggests health is a public, not just a private matter. What creates the conditions for health – by which I mean physical, social and spiritual flourishing - and how we are healthy or unhealthy goes far beyond the individual.

Why Health for Christians is a Public Issue

Because health is scientifically public not just private I believe there are a series of issues which confront us in developing and articulating a Christian discourse on health. This is where, for me as a public health professional, my practice and my values come together.

Human flourishing is a theological concern. Christians have something valuable to say about health and human flourishing into the public square. But too often our starting point has been concerned with a focus on individual suffering and coping with illness, conceptualising social inequality as a justice issue rather than linking it explicitly with health. If social justice is part of human flourishing, we are missing something when we do not explicitly consider the social justice aspects of health in our theologies of health. If health is public as well as private, doing theology on health needs to reckon with this much more explicitly than it has.

For me, there are some particular things that a Christian view on health can bring to the table in understanding the health of the public, but there are challenges in applying some Christian theological ideas to public health issues,

The challenge of what "Health" means for Christians

As suggested above, it often feels that Catholic theology's most prominent narrative on health and healing is a narrative around suffering. The theological concept of health as personal is important and valuable, but it needs to be held in tension with a theological concept of health and flourishing as social and interpersonal, with structural elements such as access to health care, access to education and employment being every bit as important as coping with ill-health. Speaking as Christians into the issue of what 'health' is, therefore, is problematic if we keep it individualised.

Speaking beyond the individualised aspect of health is urgent. In England, our government claims to value prevention but the prevention it values is a discourse of individual 'lifestyle' interventions and exhortations which fly in the face of the scientific understanding of the social determinants of health. Similarly, we have a ten year NHS plan which proposes clinical individual solutions to problems whose causes are often social. As of 2018, 26% of the English population (15 million people) were living with long term health conditions (such as diabetes, ongoing musculoskeletal disease, stroke and heart disease) for which there is no cure. Long term conditions are more prevalent in older people (58 per cent of people over 60 compared to 14 per cent under 40) and in more deprived groups (people in the poorest social class have a 60 per cent higher prevalence than those in the richest social class, and disease is typically more severe). A growing body of research shows that management of pain by drugs is sometimes unsuccessful and many people with long term conditions experience intermittent or ongoing unresolved pain. That means poorer and older people live longer in pain and ill-health than the wealthiest.

Obviously, Christian understandings of individual coping with illness and the redemptive value of suffering have clear value here. (Ryan,2009.)

But if all we do is accept this, we leave social structures and public services which predispose the most vulnerable to ill-health uncriticed and unaddressed. I could put it even more bluntly: food deserts which constrain access to healthy food are aspects of social or structural sin (Kelly, 313.) Where peoples' agency to have the means to good health is limited, it is a public, not just a private theological issue.

How does Christian Thought on Health move beyond Individualism?

Catholic tradition has long held the value of spiritual interventions to improve a person's health, affirming the unity and integration of the human person as body and soul. It would be easy to take the view that Catholic theological discourse is primarily concerned with suffering, the vocation to care for 'the sick' and bioethical principles based on the principle of bodily integrity. These themes arguably dominate recent official Catholic teaching on health (*Pontificio Consiglio per gli Operatori Sanatori*, 2016).

But one counter to this is found in Von Balthasar's meditation on health as part of his Explorations in Theology (von Balthasar, 2014). He encourages us to see how, just as scientific models are layered, Catholic theological concepts also are or can be layered or brought together in complex rather than univocal ways. He refers to the concept of health as necessarily multi-layered. '...health cannot be a simple, univocal term but can only be an analogical concept that is variously oriented to this or that...layer of the human makeup.' (Op Cit, p660.) He goes on to define three layers (not intended to be exhaustive). First, the integrity of bodily functioning. Second, a 'vital equilibrium between.. bodily and mental life...' and between person and environment. Third, the question 'of the meaning of human existence...' (Op Cit p661-662.) These must not be juxtaposed to one another but layered on each other.

To consider specifically two concepts (suffering and service) it is possible in this light to conclude that there are strong social and relational aspects to them, and that they can sit in such a complex model of health alongside other concepts.

Catholic official teaching directly links service with suffering. The parable of the Good Samaritan, says John Paul II (1984, para 28-30) and the example of Jesus lead us directly to sensitivity and service to those who suffer. 'Self-giving is at the core of Christian anthropology'. (Ibid). The suffering of others both creates an opportunity for us to show love and a requirement to act. This is both a vocation and a gospel imperative. (Ibid.) So, added to human solidarity with those who suffer are the Christian virtues and together these create a setting for response to suffering. Compassion is the fundamentally basic human element of care for others, driven out of love. In paragraph 30 he goes on to say that Christ's words in Matthew 25:31-46 provide a final perspective on suffering: 'in ministering to one who is suffering, we are ministering ultimately to Christ. All human suffering is an opportunity to serve Christ as we ought, which will be taken into account in the Final Judgment. Human suffering is revealed to be a conduit of grace, both for the one suffering and the one who ministers.'

I would go further here. Health is not just about illness but the conditions to be healthy, so solidarity demands of us that we address these structural and social determinants. Balthasar's layered model supports this.

Engagement in health care has been an enduring aspect of the Catholic Church's self-understanding of its mission, and witnesses to those it calls the 'sick' and 'suffering'. While this encourages social engagement, it feels like social engagement is an ancillary to alleviating individual suffering. The social and structural elements of this, the focus on populations not just individuals, feel downplayed.

But if we set suffering and service in relational and vocational context, there is a direct relevance to public health – the social and structural conditions which help or hinder us being healthy are as important in mission as individual therapeutic intervention.

At the same time, helping people find meaning, and helping people respond to suffering from motives of compassion and care, can help humanise the experience of living with illness, and addressing inequality. The social and personal are intertwined. Holding in tension becomes a key theological and missional task: social and individual; public health and healthcare; illness and the determinants of health outcomes. They all link us at a fundamental level to God and to each other. In this light I believe we cannot have Christian witness on health which leaves out the social and structural aspects of what makes us healthy. There is no individual suffering and no access to healthcare issue which is not, somehow, a public or social issue for Christians.

Finding a Social Lens for Health on Catholic Social Thought

Catholic Social Teaching can be seen as a discourse on social foundations for good human health, and places health not just in individual but social context. Both Catholic Social teaching and scientific and policy discourses on determinants of health emphasise the need for equity of access to the means of good health as fundamental. For me as a Public Health professional, that means that human flourishing in social, structural and environmental context as conceptualised in Catholic Social Teaching sits alongside an individual focus on suffering to produce a more nuanced Catholic understanding of the nature of human health which chimes strongly with the scientific evidence about human health at individual and population level.

Catholic Social Thought can help address the challenge of how Christians encounter the set of ethical frameworks which are traditionally deemed to be salient in the public square on health. Many of our ethical paradigms come either from utilitarianism or from individual libertarianism. For some people, ethical frameworks used in public health are often taken from biomedical ethics. Neither of these work in the context of considering the health of populations. And I contend that they are problematic from a Christian standpoint. But there is often no clear ethical discourse to counter these.

Adopting a utilitarian ethical approach radically contradicts the Christian idea that everyone matters. An individual libertarian approach also fails because health is not just what works for the individual. Neither utilitarian nor individual libertarian philosophical stances work in public health context. The former does not sufficiently value as morally salient the most excluded minorities and the latter buys in to the falsehood that health is about what individuals do, not about social determinants. Both approaches sooner or later work against the flourishing of those who are most excluded and marginalised. Christian concepts of solidarity and the need to challenge the structural sin which prevents people becoming fully healthy provide a way of affirming both excluded minorities and the social aspects of health which libertarian and utilitarian philosophies fail to do. There is a social as well as individual aspect to human flourishing. And if that is true, as seen above, we have duties towards each other in solidarity, not just individual expectations or rights.

A simplistic individualism in some recent prevention discourse - most notably official documents which enshrine 'lifestyle' as the problem and answer and concludes everything is about individual choice -needs to be criqitued by this Christian perspective of individual and social held together.

I have often found myself turning to the principles of Catholic Social Teaching for ethical guidance in public health practice (Pennock, 2007.). Because in a health context these principles allow us to hold the individual and social in tension. This holding of both as important is something Christian social ethics can contribute to a still poorly articulated area of public health policy. These principles are:

1. The dignity of each person is the foundation of society;
2. Institutions especially governments must promote the common good of all;
3. Everyone has rights to things needed for decent life, and concomitant responsibilities towards others;
4. Human dignity and justice require that everyone has a right to participate in the life of society including the right to fair, productive and non exploitative work;
5. How those most vulnerable and excluded are included and flourish is a basic moral test;
6. Care for the sustainability of our world;
7. Solidarity with all across our human diversity;
8. The state has a positive role in promoting these and assisting citizens;

I think this provides a moral foundation for public health, and a social foundation for the Church's mission in health. Starting with the dignity of the human person because of their status in relationship with God, Catholic Social Teaching works out a series of principles which are explicitly about the just relationships needed between individual, society, neighbour and institutions such as government needed to ensure the best possible human flourishing. There is an explicit link made between life and health being gifts from God and a duty to work to create the best possible conditions for human flourishing. Health is inalienably personal, of interest to God and social all at the same time. This provides an eschatological and moral context to discourses on social determinants of health.

'Life and physical health are precious gifts entrusted to us by God. We must take reasonable care of them, taking into account the needs of others and the common good. Concern for the health of its citizens requires that society help in the attainment of living-conditions that allow them to grow and reach maturity: food and clothing, housing, health care, basic education, employment, and social (Catholic Church, 1992, p. Para 2288)

The theological considerations here remain mere outlines and a theological project to elucidate these more fully is needed. Messer (2013) has explored in detail how the nature of Christian understandings of health make them essentially about relationship with God, self and each other and how this necessarily entails being in good relationship with our bodies (and minds), and requires, as we have seen from epidemiological insight, social justice and social determinants of health (employment, education) to work for maximum human flourishing. Application of Catholic Social Teaching principles for me are a fruitful way of embedding Messer's insights in practice and policy.

Public health discourse often make use of models of health which seek to provide layers of meaning from biological up to social and environmental. Van den Hoef (2018) provides just one of these identifies aspects of a complex model of health from the Individual to the Organizational or structural.

Figure 1: A Social-Ecological Model of Health (from van den Hoef, 2018.)

SEM Level	Description
Individual	• Characteristics of an individual that influence behaviour change
Interpersonal	• Formal (and informal) social networks and social support systems that can influence individual behaviours,
Community	• Relationships among organizations, institutions, and informational networks
Organizational	• Organizations or social institutions with rules that affect how services are provided to an individual or group.
Policy/Enabling Environment	• Local, state, national and global laws and policies,

There is room for a similar model to be developed as part of a project to explore more fully how scientific and Catholic Theological understandings can enrich each other and produce a complex model of health which seeks to place scientific and theological considerations together in a way which can enable further dialogue. As a first step towards that I suggest below some of the principles which might inform such a model, taking seriously von Balthasar's challenge raised above.

Figure 2: A suggested model for dialogue

Basis of a Christian anthropology of health	1. Human health cannot be understood without relationship to the work and mission of Christ. This is the fundamental context for understanding health as relational. Health and suffering link us to our neighbour in Solidarity and to Christ through his work of redeeming us and conquering suffering. 2. Our health has biological, relational, environmental, spiritual and psychological aspects of equal salience. 3. Meaning and happiness are essential for good health, for Christians this cannot be separated from an understanding of our existence as creatures in relationship with God.
The Relational context of Health and social determinants of health are linked	4. Health is never solely individual. For good health we need good relationships with God, self and other; compassion and relationship to our fellow humans and God drives us to care for others. 5. We cannot have good health without social determinants of health working for human flourishing; this is a demand of justice to enable human flourishing.
Health is linked to the Economy of Salvation	6. Health is part of the Church's mission and links us to the God who saves. 7. The existence and mission of the Church, the Sacraments and other works of sanctification are means to support our earthly flourishing and keep good relationship with God and one another as we journey through life and beyond death.

The importance of healthcare	8. We should seek to alleviate suffering and work to improve health for all using all means we can, out of solidarity for our fellow humans.
Looking after our own health as individuals	9. We should have regard to our bodily and psychological health because our body is an important part of us (St Paul says that the love Christ has for the church is analogous to the love we should have for our own body (Eph 5.29-30)).
The nature of suffering	10. Suffering and pain can have value and meaning at the same time as being something we seek to ameliorate.

A a Christian model of public health needs to be complex; scientific and theological perspectives must sit alongside each other, work at social, structural levels and individual levels and be mutually enriching.

Conclusion

The relationship between religion and human health has been the focus of growing intensity in scientific and medical research in the last fifteen years, but not so much in social theological terms or social theological ethics.

To work in public health is, as I hope I have demonstrated, to affirm the role of social determinants and environment as part of the complex manifold which are our health outcomes. To work in public health is to affirm that the principles of justice and equity are salient in enabling a conceptualisation of health as human flourishing. To work in Public Health as a Christian is a theological task, not just an epidemiological one.

Jim McManus is Director of Public Health for Hertfordshire County Council and President of the Guild of Health and St Raphael

Note

I speak from a Catholic perspective, but not from a sense that my Catholic tradition is the right or the only or in any way a privileged voice in this gathering. I am using 'church' as shorthand for the institutional vehicles for Christianity across all our denominations whether that refers to local (parish), diocesan or national/international levels.

References

Catholic Church, 1992. *Catechism of the Catholic Church*. Vatican City: Libreria Editrice Vaticana.

Corfe, S., 2018 *What are the barriers to healthy eating in the UK?* London: Social Marketing Foundation

Fountain, D., 1999. Bringing Faith and Medicine Together. *Nucleus - Journal of the Christian Medical Fellowship*, Spring, pp. 12-18.

John Paul II, P., 1984. *On the Christian Meaning of Human Suffering*. Rome: Libreria Editrice Vaticana.

Kelly, C. M. , 2019. The Nature and Operation of Structural Sin: Additional Insights from Theology and Moral Psychology. *Theological Studies*, 80 (2) 293-327.

Marmot, M., 2010. *Fair Society, Healthy Lives: Strategic Review of Inequalities in Health in England Post 2010*, London: Institute of Health Equty.

Marmot, M., Friel, S., Houweling , T. & Taylor , S., 2008. Closing the gap in a generation: health equity through action on the social determinants of health.. *The Lancet,* Volume 372, pp. 1661-1669.

McManus, H. et al., 2012. Long-Term Survival in HIV Positive Patients with up to 15 Years of Antiretroviral Therapy. *PLOS ONE*, 7(11).

Messer, N., 2013. Flourishing Messer, Neil. *Flourishing: Health, Disease, and Bioethics in Theological Perspective*. Grand Rapids: Eerdmans.

Pennock, Michael. 2007. *Catholic social teaching: learning & living justice*. Notre Dame, Ind: Ave Maria Press.

Pontificio Consiglio per gli Operatori Sanatori, 2016. *Nuova Carta Degli Operatori Sanatori*, Roma: Libreria Editrice Vaticana.

Ryan, R., 2009. *God and the Mystery of Human Suffering*. New York: Paulist Press.

Slogrove, A. L. et al., 2018. Surviving and Thriving—Shifting the Public Health Response to HIV-Exposed Uninfected Children: Report of the 3rd HIV-Exposed Uninfected Child Workshop. *Frontiers in Pediatrics*, Volume 6, p. 157.

van den Hoef, G., 2018. *Layers of Health and Parkinson's Disease.* [Online] Available at: https://gigimsht601.weebly.com/blog/levels-of-health-and-parkinsons-disease# [Accessed 1 June 2019].

von Balthasar, H. U., 2014. Health Between Science and Wisdom. *Communio*, Fall.pp. 654 - 669.

World Health Organisation, 1946. *Preamble to the Constitution of the World Health Organization as adopted by the International Health Conference, New York*, 1946, New York: World Health Organisation.

'Moral Injury' From Military Experience

Stephen Radley

Writing in the *Lancet*, Prof Edgar Jones reminds us that our word *injury* finds its roots in the Latin word, *injura*, which simply means 'a wrong' (Jones, 1766). We have used this word to describe both physical and psychiatric injuries, but more recently the term is being applied to describe the impact which an ethical dilemma may have on an individual's health.

I am a military veteran, having served as an RAF Chaplain. During my sixteen years' service I was deployed on multiple operational tours including the land invasion of Iraq in 2003. Whilst supportive of the wars at the time, today I find our actions as a nation far harder to justify. I have received counselling through the Veterans' Mental Health Services following anxiety linked to my deployments. I have also been a researchee in two studies at King's College London studying Moral Injury as my experiences make me a likely candidate to suffer from this condition. I am grateful to one of the researchers, Anaïs Philippe, for sharing her literature review with me which has helped shape my understanding of MI. I declare this background as my experiences may introduce a bias into my analysis below.

Moral Injury (MI) is often seen to be linked to the clinical diagnosis of Post Traumatic Stress Disorder (PTSD) (Koenig et al, 1) so I begin this paper with a brief history of PTSD. Using the idea that MI cannot easily be separated from PTSD I look at some ideas surrounding culture and trauma and argue our medical diagnosis may mask issues we seek to hide from as a society. I conclude with the suggestion that MI is a helpful term in our understanding of trauma as it gives the potential to embrace the spiritual in our understanding and treatment of experiences which may be injurious to more than mind and body.

PTSD was formally defined in 1980 in the American Psychiatric Association's (ASA) Diagnostic and Statistical Manual (DSM), *DSM-III*.

The definition included four basic criteria which had to be present for a diagnosis of PTSD.

A. The existence of a recognisable stressor that would evoke significant symptoms of distress in almost anyone;
B. Re-experiencing symptoms;
C. Avoidance behaviour and feelings;
D. Arousal symptoms and behaviour.

In 1994 the definition was amended in the publication of *DSM-IV*. The revised definition includes the four criteria but the definition of the stressor (criteria A) has been broadened to include both of the following:

1. The person experienced, witnessed, or was confronted with an event or events that involved actual or threatened death or serious injury, or a threat to the physical integrity of self or others;
2. The person's response involved intense fear, helplessness, or horror.

The diagnosis requires the individual to have been exposed to a specific etiological event. Even if other symptoms are present, a diagnosis of PTSD cannot be made unless the individual has been exposed to a stressor which qualifies as 'traumatic'. This condition therefore depends on what is defined a traumatic stressor.

In *DSM-III* a qualifying stressor was one which would 'evoke significant symptoms of stress in almost anyone'. In 1987 *DSM-III-R* amended criterion A to include witnessing or learning about one's family or friends being exposed to serious danger.

The revision in 1994 saw the abolishment of the definition of a traumatic event to outside the range of normal human experience. This alteration was made for two reasons. It was unclear what constituted 'usual human experience'. A stressor outside this boundary for a wealthy American may well be within the boundary for a person in an impoverished, war torn country. Secondly, many events which triggered PTSD were far from being unusual, for example road traffic accidents or criminal assault. The 1987 amendment meant you no longer had to directly experience the trauma, rather you can also witness an event, but the individual's response must include feelings of helplessness, fear or horror. These changes meant that a stressor was no longer solely defined by criteria external to the person, but now included a definition which in part included the emotional response of the person. This is an important when considering MI, as MI focuses on an individual's emotional response.

McNally argues that these changes have contributed to a conceptual bracket creep in the definition of trauma and broadened what counts as a PTSD stressor. 'For example, a person who reacts with horror upon learning about another person's exposure to a threat would qualify as having been exposed to a Criterion A traumatic stressor' (McNally in Rosen (ed), 5). This means to qualify as a trauma survivor one only need respond with fright on learning about the misfortunes of others.

DSM-V published in 2013 addresses some of these concerns and now includes PTSD within a new chapter on 'Trauma and Stress or Related Disorders'. *DSM-IV* addressed PTSD within the chapter on anxiety disorders.

The diagnostic criteria in *DSM-V* identifies the trigger to PTSD as exposure to actual or threatened death, serious injury or sexual violation. The exposure must result from one or more of the following scenarios, in which the individual:

- directly experiences the traumatic event;
- witnesses the traumatic event in person;
- learns that the traumatic event occurred to a close family member or close friend (with the actual or threatened death being either violent or accidental); or
- experiences first-hand repeated or extreme exposure to aversive details of the traumatic event (not through media, pictures, television or movies unless work-related).

DSM-V gives a clearer definition to what might constitute a traumatic event and includes recurring exposure which could apply, for example, to first responders. Language which describes the individual's emotional response to an event (fear, helplessness or horror) has been removed as this did not prove to have any bearing when predicting the onset of PTSD. Rather *DSM-V* pays more attention to the behavioural symptoms that accompany PTSD thus removing any reference to an emotional response.

'Moral Injury' From Military Experience

A briefing paper published by the American Psychiatric Association (ASA) prior to the introduction of *DSM-V* includes a short paragraph: 'PTSD Debate within the Military'.

> 'Certain military leaders, both active and retired, believe the word "disorder" makes many soldiers who are experiencing PTSD symptoms reluctant to ask for help. They have urged a change to rename the disorder posttraumatic stress injury, a description that they say is more in line with the language of troops and would reduce stigma.
>
> But others believe it is the military environment that needs to change, not the name of the disorder, so that mental health care is more accessible and soldiers are encouraged to seek it in a timely fashion. Some attendees at the 2012 APA Annual Meeting, where this was discussed in a session, also questioned whether injury is too imprecise a word for a medical diagnosis.
>
> In *DSM-5*, PTSD will continue to be identified as a disorder.' (APA(a), 2)

The ASA argument has echoes to debates during World War 1 (WW1) and the popular name for psychiatric injury, 'shellshock'. The name 'shellshock' originated outside the medical profession and was used in the popular press to describe the unusual behaviours of those exposed to the horrors of the trenches. During the early years of WW1 anyone presenting to a medical officer with shellshock like symptoms was formerly diagnosed as 'Not yet diagnosed (nervous)'. The opposition in formerly using the term 'shellshock' surrounded the belief that a formal diagnosis of shellshock would give rise to people seeking a medical diagnosis to escape the war.

Many advocates of MI suggest the emotional toll of war on an individual cannot simply be explained by the direct experience to traumatic events as defined in *DSM-V*. Its advocates suggest that MI highlights the inadequacy of a PTSD diagnosis to reflect the moral anguish military personnel experience following a combat experience. This idea is perhaps best described by Captain Boudreau of the US Marines Corps in his accounts of the war in Iraq:

> 'On a summer evening in 2004, I participated in the search of an

isolated farmhouse... We staged our trucks out of sight from the house until darkness fell. Then we moved in with terrible speed, our engines roaring, our hearts racing, and our hands tight on loaded weapons... I watched from my vehicle as the marines knocked on the front door. A man answered and, through an interpreter, they politely explained that we needed to search the premises for weapons and bomb-making materials... The man was cooperative and amiable. There was no shouting or pushing. The marines wore friendly smiles. They stepped gently through the house and were careful to replace anything they moved. Outside, other marines chatted playfully with the kids and gave them pieces of candy. When the search was complete and nothing was found, we thanked the man and apologized for the inconvenience. It was over. Not a shot was fired, not a drop of blood or a tear was shed, and yet, as we withdrew from that farmhouse and roared off into the night, I felt something inside me begin to hurt. What can I call that hurt?' (Boudreau, 746-748)

Boudreau does not discount PTSD as a valid and important diagnosis but he is critical of its use to try and rationalise all the emotional consequences of war:

'To nearly anyone who'd care enough to listen — counsellors, doctors, ministers, peace activists, folks in the community — I would bellow again and again, "I'm hurting!" ...I came home to Massachusetts and was diagnosed with PTSD by the Department of Veterans Affairs (VA)... but inwardly I knew that the greatest pain I felt was not linked to those moments when violence was being directed at me but when I was involved in inflicting it on others. Post-traumatic stress just didn't seem to fit. So what could I call this pain? It felt a lot like guilt, so that's what I started calling it, but in the Diagnostic and Statistical Manual of Mental Disorders (DSM) under PTSD there is no mention of guilt, except for "survivor's guilt," which is about being alive while one's comrades are dead, not about harming others. There has been no official name for this type of guilt and that has struck me since getting out of the military as a significant gap in the discourse on war casualties.' (Boudreau, 746-748)

The term Moral Injury predates Gulf War 2, first being used in 1994 by

Shay when describing a condition he noted within Vietnam Veterans who had experienced a betrayal of what they believed to be morally correct behaviour. The actor for this betrayal would be someone in authority and it was found only within a high stake situation. He distinguished moral injury from PTSD. Since Shay's initial observations the term has been subject to much debate but there is still no consensus surrounding its definition (NATO, 1-4) although attempts have been made to define the events which could lead to MI such as by Litz et al:

> 'Potentially morally injurious events (PMIEs), such as perpetrating, failing to prevent, or bearing witness to acts that transgress deeply held moral beliefs and expectations may be deleterious in the long-term, emotionally, psychologically, behaviourally, spiritually, and socially.' (Litz et al, p.695)

Whist this definition attempts to recognise the scope within which someone may suffer from a MI, research suggests the situations which can lead to a MI are more diverse. These situations include (but not exclusively) having done the right thing but still being troubled by that action and regretting having participated in a war which the individual no longer considers to be just (Lee, Jones, 1766). The emotions and feeling specifically related to MI are guilt and shame (Marek et al, 3).

A difficulty with recognising MI is found within the clinical outcomes which can mirror those for PTSD: Depression, Anxiety, Substance Abuse, Sleep Problems, Relationship Problems, Headaches/Pain, Physical, Disability, Unemployment, (Koenig et al, 2). Koenig argues the dynamics involved in MI include: guilt, shame, moral concerns, feeling betrayed, loss of trust, difficulty forgiving, loss of meaning/purpose, self-condemnation. If you have a religious belief these dynamics can also include a loss of religious faith/hope.

Summerfield argues that the roots of contemporary mental health practice can be found in the European Enlightenment and Cartesian assumptions that the inner world of the mind had a separate realm outside the body, which could be studied (Summerfield, 54). Psychiatric science, in investigating human pain and suffering, sought to convert it into technical problems which could be understood and standardized. Bracken argues psychiatric knowledge is seen as neutral, objective, disinterested and universally applicable (Bracken, 733).

The period of the European Enlightenment challenged the authority of the religious establishment and the received wisdom of religious revelation on which Western society had been founded (Bracken, 733). Until this period human suffering had been explained and accepted as 'the will of God' (Summerfield in Kirmayer et al (ed), 233). With the decline in influence of religion, the understanding of suffering became a problem for scientists to solve. Summerfield argues that these beginnings have led to a major feature of twentieth century culture as in the medicalized ways of seeing which have displaced religion as the source for explanations about life and the vocabulary of distress. 'The impact of violence and other morally shocking types of suffering are now framed through the morally neutral sciences of memory and psychology' (Summerfield in Kirmayer et al, 233).

By using Descartes method of doubt, the European Enlightenment and science as heirs of this model have destroyed the certainty they sought to establish. A non deceiving God has been replaced with self-reflexivity leading to uncertainty, not certainty. The seeds of uncertainly, planted during the modern period, appear to have grown into an ever more powerful concept. This has led to a removal of the foundations on which a stable 'way of life' was founded. The Western societies have experienced a move away from religious and other belief systems, which offered meaningful frameworks to encounter death and suffering (Giddens cited Bracken, 740).

Cultures require a framework of understanding and the removal of religion as Western society's system of meaning has led to a cultural expectation that experiencing a distressing event will lead to a psychiatric injury. McNally identifies both a paradox of PTSD and the influence of culture on how we interpret events:

> 'The central paradox of PTSD is that psychologically traumatizing events – as distinct from physically traumatizing ones – must be cognitively appraised for their impact to be felt... A psychic trauma carries its force through the meaning the event has for the person. The proximal cause of PTSD may be how the person interprets the meaning of the stressor. And how one interprets the event may, in turn, be influenced by historic and cultural factors. For example, although witnessing the violent death of another person is currently deemed a Criterion A stressor, attending public executions has often been a popular form of family entertainment throughout history.' (McNally in Rosen (ed), 5).

DSM-V recognises the impact of cultural experience within any diagnosis and experience although this recognition is limited to behaviours:

> 'Different cultures and communities exhibit or explain symptoms in various ways. Because of this, it is important for clinicians to be aware of relevant contextual information stemming from a patient's culture, race, ethnicity, religion or geographical origin. For example, uncontrollable crying and headaches are symptoms of panic attacks in some cultures, while difficulty breathing may be the primary symptom in other cultures.' (ASA(b), 1)

Herman argues that there has always been a tendency to push traumatic events out of both an individual's consciousness but also out of social consciousness. To study the effects of traumatic events, particularly ones such as rape, torture and sexual abuse, means having to face the capacity for evil within humanity. She argues that:

> 'To hold traumatic reality in consciousness requires a social context that affirms and protects the victim and joins victim and witness in a common alliance. For the individual victim, this social context is created by relationships with friends, lovers, and family. For the larger society, the social context is created by political movements that give voice to the disempowered.' (Hermen, 1992, cited Bracken, 9)

Herman believes that the discourse on trauma has emerged because of various political movements. The rise of feminism has allowed a better understanding of the effects of sexual violence and the large scale social movement which opposed the Vietnam war allowed for the critical examination of the effects of wartime experiences. Prior to this, she argues, government propaganda promoted the idea that battlefield experience had a positive and maturing influence on the individual. The negative way the Vietnam war was viewed allowed psychiatrists to examine the negative effects of wartime experience. She concludes PTSD has always existed but remained hidden until recently.

Herman's argument fails to account for the changes in cultural thinking central to the post-modern narrative, although her observation that traumatic experiences force us to engage with the potential capacity of 'evil' within humanity is an attempt to find a new narrative to explain suffering.

I find Herman's argument persuasive when considering the nature of PTSD and I believe it can be extended to MI. Could it be that our diagnoses of trauma have hidden a deeper sickness within society which sees war as a necessary and positive exploit? If this is true it opens the possibility that the psychiatric outcomes of war are more than a 'disorder' but may be injurious to both mind and spirit. An example of the UK's embrace of war can be seen through the festivals of remembrance held annually in November. Poppies are sold to support those injured in war and churches across the nation hold remembrance service to commemorate those who have died 'fighting for their country'. Yet this commemoration does not lead to movements which seek to change individual and societal behaviours which would make war less likely. The white poppy movement (established in the 1930s) is an attempt to change behaviours but does not attract the same level of support by Church or State as the red poppy movement which simply remembers military personnel who have died in war. Conservative MP, Rt. Hon. Johnny Mercer called white poppies "attention seeking rubbish" in 2018.[1]

Along with the links to PTSD, MI has also been related to other mental health disorders such as depression and anxiety (Koening). The challenges when trying to disentangle the concept of MI from other psychopathologies and the difficulties of ascribing a label to it means it attracts a lot of debate and research. A further problem is identifying what constitutes moral. Could you suffer from MI simply because you did something you felt to be wrong, which another would consider to be right? Some scholars suggest the term moral is not helpful and would rather it be replaced with terms such as spiritual or emotion (Drescher, 8).

As a Christian I would argue moral injury is a useful adjunction to our understanding of psychiatric trauma which has, as its focus, the mind. Whilst the term is debated, and the reality of MI considered, such debates do at least force us to consider the possibility that holistic care should embrace more than mind and body. In so doing it helps us consider the spiritual. It may be that spiritual injury is a better term for MI. If nothing else, the concept of MI appears to be useful in helping find a more holistic approach to treatment from traumatic events. Dresher et al note that the treatment of MI should be collaborative between mental health providers and chaplains.

'Veterans benefit when clergy and mental health providers work collaboratively to provide optimal care. Issues of guilt, shame, remorse, and forgiveness related to combat where injury or death were inflicted, witnessed, or not prevented will inevitably arise when veterans speak with mental health providers and with religious professionals. These spiritual struggles and health symptoms are relevant for both mental health treatment and for spiritual care.' (Dresher, 59)

In conclusion, the recognition of MI as a spiritual consequence of war is a helpful term to embrace. Although the APA warn against the use of the term 'injury' to describe the psychological effects of war on a person, the meaning of the word 'injura' as 'a wrong' may make it an appropriate word to use. Shellshock gained popular recognition before being formally adopted into medical vocabulary; the same may be true for MI.

The term 'moral' is too imprecise to adequately describe the feelings of guilt and shame associated with this condition and a better word might be 'spiritual'. This places the condition firmly within a framework of understanding, but it should be remembered that PTSD is also placed within a framework of meaning. As Young states:

'The disorder [PTSD] is not timeless, nor does it possess an intrinsic unity. Rather it is glued together by the practices, technologies, and narratives with which it is diagnosed, studied, treated, and represented and by the various interests, institutions, and moral arguments that mobilized these efforts and resources.' (Young, 5).

There is a lot of debate about whether MI is a real condition and its links to PTSD. As a Christian I would argue that such debate is fruitless, as any action will have an effect on body, mind and spirit, and so will be interlinked. The development of the term MI is exciting, as it provides a new framework through which our care towards those who suffer in body, mind and spirit can become more holistic. It may also help us to face ideas and practices within society which we might otherwise avoid or ignore.

The Revd Stephen Radley is Chief Operations Officer at The Guild of Health and St Raphael, and runs his own business promoting good mental health.

Questions for discussion

1. The contributor argues that the nature of psychiatric injury can at least in part be explained through society's loss of a Christian narrative which gives some meaning to suffering. To what extent do you feel this may or may not be true?

2. Do you feel Moral Injury is a useful term which has the potential to provide a more holistic treatment for those who have experienced things which have affected their mind; or do you feel this an unhelpful term which provides the potential for people to 'jump on a bandwagon' when they have been involved in things that, as an individual, they now feel to be wrong?

Note

1. https://www.bbc.co.uk/news/uk-45971456

References

American Psychiatric Association, 2013(a) *DSM-V Collection, Posttraumatic Stress Disorder*, [Internet], https://www.psychiatry.org/File%20Library/Psychiatrists/Practice/DSM/APA_DSM-5-PTSD.pdf

American Psychiatric Association, 2013(b), *DSM-V Cultural Concepts*, [Internet] https://www.psychiatry.org/File%20Library/Psychiatrists/Practice/DSM/APA_DSM_Cultural-Concepts-in-DSM-5.pdf

Bracken, Patrick J. (2001) Post-modernity and post-traumatic stress disorder. *Social Science and Medicine*. 53: 733-743

Boudreau T. *The Morally Injured*. Mass Rev. 2011;52(3):746–54. [Internet]. http://www.massreview.org/sites/default/files/Boudreau.pdf

Drescher, K. D., Nieuwsma, J. A., Smales, P. J., 2013, *Morality & Moral Injury: Insights from Theology & Health Science*. Reflective Practice

Drescher KD, Foy DW, Kelly C, Leshner A, Schutz K, Litz B. An exploration of the viability and usefulness of the construct of moral injury in war veterans. *Traumatology* (Tallahass Fla). 2011;17(1):8–

13
Giddens, A. (1991). *Modernity and self identity. Self and society in the late modern age.* Cambridge: Polity Press cited Bracken (2001), p. 740

Hermen, J (1992), *Trauma and Recovery. The aftermath of violence – from domestic violence to political terror.* New York: Basic Books.

Jones E. (2018), The art of medicine Moral injury in time of war. *Lancet* [Internet]. 391:1766

Kirmayer, Laurence, Lemelson, Robert, Barad, Mark (eds) (2007), *Understanding Trauma. Integrating Biological, Clinical, and Cultural Perspectives*, Cambridge: Cambridge University Press

Koenig HG, Ames D, Youssef NA, Oliver RJP, Min D, Volk F, et al. Screening for Moral Injury: The Moral Injury Symptom Scale – Military Version Short Form. Mil Med. 2018;00(May):1–7

Litz BT, Stein N, Delaney E, Lebowitz L, Nash WP, Silva C, et al. Moral injury and moral repair in war veterans: A preliminary model and intervention strategy. Clin Psychol Rev [Internet]. 2009;29(8):695–706. Available from: http://dx.doi.org/10.1016/j.cpr.2009.07.003

Lee P., *Blair's Just War: Iraq and the Illusion of Morality.* London, UK: Palgrave Macmillan; 2012.

Marek S. Kopacz and Janet M. McCarten Vance CG. A Preliminary Study for Exploring Different Sources of Guilt in a Sample of Veterans Who Sought Chaplaincy Services. *Military Psychology* 2015: 27(1):1–8

North Atlantic Treaty Organisation Science and Technology Organisation., 2018, Human Factors and Medicine Panel. Moral Decisions and Military Mental Health. STO Technical Report.

Philippe, A. (2018), Does religious belief mediate the effect of moral injury after potentially morally injurious events for military personnel. Unpublished dissertation, Kings College London.

Rosen, Gerald (ed) (2004), *Posttraumatic Stress Disorder. Issues and Controversies.* Chichester: John Wiley & Sons

Summerfied, Derek (2001), The Invention of post-traumatic stress disorder and the social usefulness of a psychiatric category, *BMJ*, 322: 95-98

Young, Alan (1995), *The Harmony of Illusions. Inventing Post-Traumatic Stress Disorder*, New Jersey: Princeton University Press

Why Mother Church Should Care About Her Children's Bodies

Jacqueline R Cameron

Befriending the body

'The Body of Christ...' Most of us hear these words every week; most churchgoers have at least heard of the doctrine of Incarnation. We are pretty good at focusing on the spiritual benefits of Jesus's life and ministry, but how often do we stop to think about the profound implications of Jesus's physicality and how it affected his earthly life and ministry? How often do we stop to think about our own experience of physicality and how it shapes our identity, our spiritual life and our ministries?

To what extent might cultivating a sense of awe and gratitude for our bodies, or embracing a deeper appreciation of the interplay between the physical and the spiritual broaden our vision and spark creativity in mission?

Some—both within and outside the Church—think that Christianity is all about the soul, and that the only significance of Jesus's saving life and work was to provide spiritual benefits.

This neglect of the body stands alongside a still damaging history, during which Christian individuals and groups have practised overt bodily abuse and have considered it a necessary part of faithful Christian living. At times, this abuse and neglect has been focused on attempts to control or extinguish sexual desire, but it was often rooted in a general distaste for all things physical, owing to a mistaken belief that the physical was somehow opposed to the spiritual. At best, this has left us with an impoverished appreciation of the body, but it often lingers in the form of deep suspicion and secret shame about our own bodies today.

This is even more tragic as we consider the high prevalence of poor physical health, poor body image, and rampant body-related psychological and social suffering in the world at large.

As she considers this growing epidemic of body dissatisfaction, theologian Paula Gooder observes, "It sometimes feels as though the Christian response is currently a ringing silence."[1] She goes on to note that "a general silence on the body's importance…can easily suggest that the body is something to be controlled not loved; ignored and overcome rather than cherished…. It is not difficult to see from teaching on abstinence and on sex, that Christians become embarrassed by or hostile to embodiment…."[2]

But there is no part of Christian theology, worship or mission that does not embrace the fullness of human living—physical, relational, emotional, intellectual, and spiritual. Scripture, sacraments, theology and history all tell of a continuing dance, or collision, between the divine and the physical or created world. And because we are physical beings, all our perceptions of and interactions with those things that are outside us are *mediated* through the physical body.

Words are spoken. Eardrums and tiny bones vibrate; nerves spark and fire. A sound is perceived. Memories are stirred; new thoughts take form. Hormones, neurotransmitters and other body chemicals surge and flow and stop and start over again. Heartbeats speed up and slow down. Muscles twitch and relax. Joy, fear, grief or hope might be generated or curbed.

The very same words spoken as poetry or set to music might stir up an entirely different physical, emotional, and, of course, spiritual, experience. Images, colour, movement, sound and smell might intersect with previous experience and confirm or reshape it, or might shock us into an entirely new perception of God and the world.

All of this *physical* activity mediates and facilitates—and sometimes impedes—*spiritual* perceptions, beliefs and experiences as well. Sometimes these experiences help us to connect with other people or with God in a new way. And still, so much remains shrouded in mystery!

Jesus walked and talked and preached and taught and fed and healed and befriended people—and he did all of this in order to invite them into a healed relationship with God.

For those of us who worship God the Creator, follow in the footsteps of Jesus the Healer and believe that the Spirit still blows new life into the world, all of this messy and mysterious physicality can open up a rich array of possibility for creative and compassionate ministry.

But what is clear is that the world needs Jesus' followers to engage in Jesus-style ministry that tends to the whole person—including the body. As one of our post-communion prayers puts it, "we offer and present to you, O Lord, ourselves, our souls and our bodies, to be a reasonable, holy and living sacrifice..."[3]

Theological foundations

In Scripture, we read the stories of the faithful who have gone before us. We gain wisdom from their mistakes and are encouraged by their faithfulness. In liturgy, we encounter God again and again through words, music, senses and movement. In theology, we attempt to explore and to express the deep mysteries of God in ways that make sense in our own time and context. And of course, in order fully to engage in all of these spiritual activities, we need a body!

The biblical record opens with stories of God-breathed creation. In these stories God takes a risk—a beautiful risk—in calling forth a mind-boggling array of living creatures, plants, planets, water, and air. There are stars and starfish, blazing sun and deepest midnight, amoebas and elephants, orbits and tides. Humans are given the capacity for loving relationship with one another and with God.

It is all physical. And God called it good.

The Bible is filled with very human stories of illness and healing, hunger and feasting, love and grief. In Jesus, we find God's most humanly palpable presence. Like us, he entered the world through the pain and labour of a pregnant woman. During his earthly ministry, he healed and taught and fed. He also suffered physical hunger and pain, exhaustion, betrayal, and a brutal death.

The New Testament writers insist that Jesus' resurrection was not merely a spiritual phenomenon—Jesus's resurrected life included a physical body. St Paul proclaims an indissoluble link between Jesus's life and death and bodily resurrection, and our faith that God will raise us as well. Paul, of course, is a central and still controversial figure in Christian thought and life. Many Christians believe that he had a low view of the body and that his writings strongly extolled the value of the spiritual life over—and sometimes at the expense of—the physical. Though a thorough exploration of Paul's thought is beyond the scope of this paper, Paula Gooder has made a strong argument for a very different reading of Paul in her book *Body: Biblical Spirituality for the Whole Person*.

Looking closely at Romans and 1 Corinthians, she builds a careful and persuasive case for Paul holding a very high view of the body. In fact, if we follow her lead and find ourselves persuaded about the centrality of the body in faithful Christian living, we would find our identity, worship and ministry profoundly transformed, and would be far better equipped to love and serve the world in God's name.

In Romans 12:1-2, Paul writes:

"I urge you therefore, brothers and sisters, through the mercies of God, to present your bodies as a sacrifice, living, holy and well-pleasing to God, which is your reasonable worship, and not to be moulded to this age, but to be transfigured by the renewal of the mind, that you may ascertain what is the will of God—the good and well-pleasing and perfect." (Gooder's own translation)[4]

She argues that in Romans 1-11, Paul "laid out the full detail of what he perceives to be the 'mercies of God'. In chapters 12-16, he invited the Romans to respond to those mercies. His summary of how the Romans should respond...involved two actions: that they should present their bodies (v.1), and should be transformed or transfigured by the renewal of the mind (v.2)."[5]

Reading the health needs around us

In the centuries that have elapsed since Christianity's foundation, health care in the UK has largely become the responsibility of the state. But neither the state nor Christian outreach has been successful in so promoting human thriving that diabetes, heart disease, hypertension and other chronic conditions are prevented in the first place. Obesity is the most visible of these maladies, and generates much of the illness sapping life, productivity and joy from millions of people in England. The risks of disease and disability, and the risk of several cancers, increase in line with surplus weight.[6]

The proportion of the population affected by obesity has grown steadily, and now includes children. One in ten children arrive in Primary School already obese, but by the time they leave one is five is obese.[7] The Government's Childhood Obesity Strategy updated in

January 2017[8] provides a stark assessment of their future health.

> "Today nearly a third of children aged 2 to 15 are overweight or obese and younger generations are becoming obese at earlier ages and staying obese for longer... obesity doubles the risk of dying prematurely. Obese adults are seven times more likely to become a type 2 diabetic than adults of a healthy weight which may cause blindness or limb amputation. And not only are obese people more likely to get physical health conditions like heart disease, they are also more likely to be living with conditions like depression"

The burden falls most heavily on poorer children. Five year olds from the poorest income groups are twice as likely to be obese compared to their most well off counterparts, and by age 11 they are three times as likely to be obese.[9]

Apart from the powerful and direct links between obesity and disease, the condition takes a heavy toll on wider measures of "wellbeing". Being overweight also leads to bullying. The What About YOUth (WAY) Survey 2014 showed that 46% of 15-year-old girls and 23% of boys thought that they were "too fat" and of those, 34% said that others had made fun of them because of their weight.[10]

An All Party Parliamentary Group on Body Image (carried out in 2012) found that two out of three people in the UK – including children as young as five – are unhappy with their body.[11] Poor body image increases the risk of anxiety and depression, and reduces self confidence, and critically, willingness to take part in physical activity. In a 2012 Girl Guides study on Girls' Attitudes found that 23% of girls aged 7-21 said that they did not participate in exercise because of poor body image even though 62% of them believed that exercise was an important part of being healthy.[12] Young people and adults who perceive themselves to be overweight are also less likely to be physically active, and, when older, are more likely to be isolated from their communities.[13]

The deprivation/inactivity cycle

Social deprivation also has the capacity to damage people's bodies. It is associated with reduced life expectancy (DFLE); inequality in DFLE between affluent and deprived areas increased during the first decade of the 21st Century.[14] Intriguingly, the perception in people of their own relative low social rank is associated with increased caloric intake and weight gain.[15] Social deprivation is also associated with depression and a number of harmful habits such as smoking.[16] The All Party Parliamentary Group on Hunger estimates that up to three million children in the UK are at risk of inadequate nutrition during school holidays, resulting in impairment of their fitness and academic performance, especially in comparison with better-off peers.[17]

The physical inactivity exacerbated by social deprivation and overweight constitutes a potent threat to health and wellbeing. There is growing evidence that sedentary behaviour might be even more dangerous than obesity. Sitting for long periods damages practically every system in the body and appears to be linked to depression and other mental health problems.

Physical activity works

Just as physical inactivity can seriously harm health and wellbeing, so activity and sport can have a critical role in restoring them. It is a remedy, moreover, within the grasp of a national organisation such as the Church, with its network of volunteers and buildings.

There's strong evidence from research showing the power of exercise and activity. One study of English school children found that physically fit children from deprived areas were exempt from the overweight and obesity otherwise associated with socially deprived areas.[18] The Government's childhood obesity report observes that physical activity improves the muscle and bone strength of children, their health and fitness, quality of sleep and academic performance, as well as maintenance of healthy weight.[19] Several studies in both girls and boys have found vigorous activity and increased fitness associated with significantly improved self esteem.[20]

The activities necessary to provide these benefits need not be beyond the capacity of church-run programmes. Interrupting sedentary behaviour with even short bouts of activity – as little as two minutes of brisk walking for example – is enough to improve blood flow, energy and concentration. Targeting the least active people, ie. those who currently engage in physical activity for less than 30 minutes a week, is likely to produce the biggest gains in health.

Exercise and recreation are about much more than weight management. They may also help to reduce the risk of anxiety, depression and suicide in children and adolescents.[21] One 2006 study proposed that physical activity and sport may help to reduce depression in adolescent girls by improving physical self-concept and self-esteem, regardless of weight or perceptions of appearance.[22] It may also help to regulate or curb destructive behaviours such as smoking, gambling, drug use and overeating.[23]

The potential benefits of physical activity and sport are not confined to the young. Age UK estimates that over half of people aged 75 or more live alone, and that more than 200,000 older people in the UK have not had a conversation with friends or family in over a month. Appropriately modified physical activity and sport can improve emotional and social as well as physical wellbeing.[24]

In his book *Every Body Matters*, Gary Thomas tells the story of Karen, a young mother, once an accomplished volleyball player, who lost her confidence and gained weight during the stress of adopting a child. She overcame anxiety and went to an open volleyball session. As she continued to play week by week, Karen began to feel stronger, healthier and more energetic, so that eventually her relationship with God also took on a new vitality.[25]

Get moving

Without intervention from organisations such as the Church, the potential benefit of physical activity will remain locked up. The Chief Medical Office for England recommends 30 minutes of moderate to vigorous physical activity for adults on most days of the week (60 minutes for children aged 5-15).

Despite this well-advertised message, Sport England calculates that more than one in four people in England (28 per cent) do less than 30 minutes of physical activity *a week*. The Active People Survey 2014/15 showed that only 6% of men and 4% of women whose activity was measured, met the official recommendations.[26]

It's a similar picture among children. The Health Survey for England showed that fewer than a quarter of boys and only a fifth of girls aged 5 to 15 met official guidelines of sixty minutes of physical activity every day.[27]

But according to Sport England, there's a significant public desire to be more active. In a study of London, it estimated this "latent demand" at fully two-thirds of all people.[28] The urgent need and evident demand for physical activity, give the Church a precious opportunity to minister, to heal, and to evangelise.

Can the Church make a difference?

If we look at just one diocese – London – we see the Church already making a difference. Sport England has found about 40,000 people attending church or church-school affiliated sport or physical activity sessions in an average week, including 640 regular church-based events, and a further 245 sponsored by churches but taking place elsewhere. They include mainstream sports as well as dance exercise, aerobics, martial arts and yoga, and foster above average attendance by girls, women and older people, all at risk of dangerously low levels of physical activity.

However, Sport England's report concluded that there was significant spare capacity in church and school facilities, and that better designed programmes, wider collaboration and more effective communication were needed.[29]

There are several outstanding examples of parish-based activity programmes in London. St John's, Hoxton has transformed the health, lifestyle, eating habits and self-esteem of women attending a Lenten group, and has developed sustainable models for other parishes to run fitness and exercise classes. All Souls, Langham Place, offers an extensive array of activities ranging from pilates, table tennis and badminton, to touch rugby and football at venues across London.[30] St John's, Southall, used a mobile cage to provide young people on local estates, most of them Muslim, to play football. More than fifty young men from a local council estate took part in the football project run by St Alban's, Fulham. Many parishes now offer weekly yoga classes.

The diocesan-wide London Sports Ministry Partners Networks works with many parachurch organisations to deliver sport and physical activity. To name just a couple, Ambassadors Football uses the sport to help marginalised men stuck in cycles of unemployment, homelessness and addiction, and improves the physical fitness and employability of disadvantaged fathers. Kick London, works in 26 church schools in London delivering a range of physical activities, including Street Dance and the PE National Curriculum, encouraging children to attend parish-based football and dance academies.

Throughout England, the Church faces a huge challenge to engage young people. A YFC report "GenZ – Rethinking Culture" found that almost half of young people did not believe in the existence of God, and only 18% would be interested in finding out more. The same report found that more than half of the same sample cited sport and exercise as one of their top five spare-time activities.[31]

Physical activity is critical to our health and wellbeing as individuals and communities. It also offers a way for the church to engage that society. It will not be alone in the effort. In 2015 the Government published its sport strategy *Sporting Future: A New Strategy for an Active Nation*[32] seeking to use sport and physical activity to improve mental and physical health, to develop individuals and communities, and to benefit the economy. Funding decisions will be made on the basis of how programmes can meet those targets. In 2016, Sport England published its own strategy, *Towards an Active Nation*, setting out how it would spend £250 million to combat inactivity.[33] With its network of parishes, halls, schools and volunteers, the Church could help to meet an urgent need and greatly expand its ministry at the same time.

Why mother church should care about her children's bodies

Jesus preached and taught, but he also healed and fed his followers. Throughout history, from monastic hospitality to ancient and modern hospitals, from cancer support groups to food banks, ministries of healing and feeding have always been an integral part of Christian identity and practice.

There's more at stake for the Church even than the illness, isolation and distress caused by neglect of our bodies. By developing a livelier appreciation and respect for the mystery and complexity of the body, we will honour the record of scripture, enrich our encounter with God in worship, and engage more robustly with theology. Our pastoral care and creative ministry will be expanded. We will become more like Jesus.

If statistics are to be believed, our friends and neighbours are desperate for opportunities to get active, to discover their bodies' strength and ability, to let go of body-related shame, to have some fun, and to connect with others.

As individuals, not everyone will be able to run a sport programme or organise a complex physical health ministry, although most of us could do something—even if it's as simple as hosting a walk before or after a church service.

We experience God's love and healing through worship, through reflection on Scripture, and through the giving and receiving of compassionate care. By offering expanded opportunities for physical activity and sport, we can help to heal illness, stress, inequality and loneliness.

This is sacramental work. When we baptise, marry, anoint, or celebrate the Eucharist, we are transported across a living yet still mysterious bridge between the physical and the spiritual. When we deepen our appreciation of our own bodies, when we care for them more lovingly, and when we invite our friends and neighbours to do the same, we honour God the Creator, we follow more closely in the footsteps of Jesus the Healer, and we join in the life of the Spirit, whose life-restoring breath flows through us all.

> *Jacqueline Cameron is a physician and assistant professor in the Departments of Internal Medicine and Preventive Medicine at Rush University Medical Center in Chicago, and a member of the Ethics Consultation Service in the Department of Religion, Health and Human Values. She is an Episcopal priest in the Diocese of Chicago and serves as a consultant for clergy wellness in the Diocese of London.*

Questions for Discussion

1. In Christian history, how has the Church valued or not valued the body, for example (as Gooder put it), treating the body as 'something to be controlled, not loved; ignored and overcome rather than cherished'?

2. How do you feel about your own body? Do you see it as something awe-inspiring? Something disappointing or shameful? Something with which God the creator is well-pleased? Merely temporary and therefore not terribly important or valuable?

3. Do people with diseases that may have been made worse by lifestyle choices deserve what they get?

4. What are some of the physical needs of the people in your parish or community? Can you think of a few creative ideas of how you or your church might begin to address some of these needs?

Notes

1. Gooder, P. (2016) *Body: Biblical spirituality for the whole person.* London: SPCK, p. 3.
2. Gooder, p. 5, 6.

3. Common Worship, p. 294.
4. Gooder, p. 104.
5. Gooder, p. 104.
6. HSCIC 2016 p.6; http://content.digital.nhs.uk/catalogue/PUB20562/obes-phys-acti-diet-eng-2016-rep.pdf.
7. HSCIC 2016, p.15.
8. https://www.gov.uk/government/publications/childhood-obesity-a-plan-for-action/childhood-obesity-a-plan-for-action.
9. https://www.gov.uk/government/uploads/system/uploads/attachment_data/file/216370/dh_128210.pdf
10. What About YOUth (WAY) Survey 2014
11. All Party Parliamentary Group on Body Image, 2012.
12. PA and Body Image in Children, Make Time 2 Play, July 2013 and All Party Parliamentary Group (APPG) on Body Image 2013 and YMCA: Be Real Campaign (berealcampaign.co.uk).
13. PA and Body Image in Children, 2013.
14. Smith MP et al. Health Stat Q. 2010 Winter;(48):36-57. Inequalities in disability-free life expectancy by rea deprivation: England, 2001-04 and 2005-08.
15. Cheon, BK et al. Proc Natl Acad Sci USA; 2017 Jan 3;114(1):72-77. doi: 10.1073/pnas.1607330114. Epub 2016 Dec 19.
16. Denny S et al. Int J Equity Health. The association between socioeconomic deprivation and secondary school students' health: findings from a latent class analysis of a national adolescent health survey. 2016 Jul 16;15(1):109. doi: 10.1186/s12939-016-0398-5.
17. http://www.frankfield.co.uk/upload/docs/437488_TSO_Britain's%20not-so-hidden%20hunger.pdf
18. Nevill AM, Duncan MJ, Lahart I, Sandercock G. Modelling the association between weight status and social deprivation in English school children: Can physical activity and fitness affect the relationship? Ann Hum Biol 2016 Nov; 43(6):497-504. Epub 2015 Dec 1.
19. https://www.gov.uk/government/publications/childhood-obesity-a-plan-for-action/childhood-obesity-a-plan-for-action
20. PA and Body Image in Children.
21. The Mental Health of Children and Young People in England, December 2016; p.5 (https://www.gov.uk/government/uploads/system/uploads/attachment_data/file/575632/Mental_health_of_children_in_England.pdf).
22. Dishman, Rod et al (May 2006) PA and sport may help decrease

depression symptoms in adolescent girls by improving physical self-concept and self-esteem; *Health Psychology* Vol 25(3): 396-407. (http://dx.doi.org/10.1037/0278-6133.25.3.396).

23. Medicine and Science in Sports and Exercise.

24. https://www.nice.org.uk/news/article/nice-calls-on-third-sector-and-public-bodies-to-work-together-to-prevent-loneliness-in-older-people?utm_source=NICE+Newsletter&utm_campaign=3304dc5e4c-NICE+News+December+2016&utm_medium=email&utm_term=0_8b79289514-3304dc5e4c-168884953

25. Thomas, G. *Every Body Matters*. (Grand Rapids, MI: Zondervan, 2011)

26. According to Sport England, 38% of adults in London reported participating in sport at least once in the previous week. See London Sport Insight Portal (https://data.londonsport.org); some information from Active People Survey (Sport England).

27. Health Survey for England 2015, p. 28 and 30.

28. Sport England, Active Lives Survey, pub January 2017; https://data.londonsport.org/dataset/borough-physical-activity-and-sport-profiles-2017?utm_source=London%20Sport%20subscribers&utm_campaign=3d5b561a52-EMAIL_CAMPAIGN_2017_05_05&utm_medium=email&utm_term=0_f124d59b59-3d5b561a52-245050549

29. T Crabbe, F McGee and G Dash, Sport England: Sport and the Church of England Research, Final Report, February 2015.

30. http://www.allsouls.org/Groups/106371/Networks/Sports/Sports.aspx

31. https://yfc.co.uk/rethinkingculture/

32. https://www.gov.uk/government/publications/sporting-future-a-new-strategy-for-an-active-nation

33. https://www.sportengland.org/news-and-features/news/2016/may/19/sport-england-triples-investment-in-tackling-inactivity/

Home Truths

A Theological Reflection on Social Housing

Mike Long

This Forum article will identify elements of a theological contribution to issues of social housing, with particular reference to the publication by the Commission on Social Housing of the charity Shelter: *A Vision for Social Housing*.[1] It summarises the history of social housing, the nature of the issues being faced and their causal factors, and identifies theological points of engagement.

There is a growing consensus that the housing system is failing. The scale of the problem is manifest across the country with more than one million families on housing waiting lists[2] and 300,000 people classed as homeless.[3] The reasons for this are many: the relative unaffordability of housing for purchase; the high rental values in the private rented sector; and the paucity of housing built, especially social housing. Much of this is driven by high asset prices, particularly in the south-east of England, in major cities and popular rural locations such as coastal towns.

A history of social housing

Social housing in Britain was introduced as a remedy for the expensive and poor housing conditions of many urban tenants. Private renting was insecure, overcrowded and could not deliver decent, affordable housing for the local population. The first introduction of council-funded housing was in 1869 in Vauxhall, Liverpool, where a progressive local authority, with an impressive track record in improving public health, constructed 146 tenement dwellings following legislation that allowed municipalities to borrow at subsidised rates from government.[4] Initiatives were also taken by Victorian philanthropists such as Octavia Hill and the Peabody Trust, who constructed homes for the local working-classes, but in time often ran into financial difficulties. The first council 'estate' was built in 1900 in Bethnal Green in East London.[5] Financial constraints meant that rents were too high for those the housing had originally been intended for, and more affluent residents made up the tenant base.[6] By the early years of the twentieth century a plethora of local authority schemes were being tried in inner-cities, suburbs and rural areas.

Between the wars the cities grew enormously as new suburbs were created: Birmingham built 51,000 homes – the highest number – during this period alone.[7] Town planning emerged as a distinct discipline. The housing losses caused by the war led to a huge expansion in house building. A wave of new towns emerged, and Labour and Conservative governments vied with each other to build the greatest number of council homes. Such housing was intended for the ordinary working person or family and many people took pride in obtaining their first tenancy. In 1953 a peak was reached with 229,000 council homes out of a total figure of 318,000 constructed during that year.[8] The changing nature of housing need, with falling household sizes as well as aesthetic reasons, led to the construction of high rises from the late 1950s and, a few years later, the introduction of prefabricated Large Panel System construction. Innovative designs featuring 'cities in the sky' with elaborate walkways became common features, but in many cases became notorious for poor amenities, design flaws, crime and anti-social behaviour.

Many churches in the post-war period became involved in setting up housing associations, involving small-scale developments on ecclesiastical land or purchasing run-down properties to renovate for let. In the area near Grenfell Tower, and in addition to Octavia Housing, the Notting Hill Housing Trust and Paddington Churches Housing (now merged to form Notting Hill Genesis) remain important examples.[9] This tradition continues to the present day across the country.

Since the Thatcherite revolution of the 1980s many former council homes have been bought by their tenants, and a significant proportion subsequently let for profit. Since the 1990s much council housing stock has been offloaded onto a variety of bodies including housing associations, to manage such properties. A steady increase in home ownership over many decades peaked in 2003 and has declined since, accompanied by a significant expansion in the private rented sector (PRS).[10]

A failing housing system

The impetus for the Shelter commission was the Grenfell Tower fire in west London which claimed 72 lives. A common refrain in the fire's aftermath, and echoed among many respondents, was the experience of being ignored by those responsible for property maintenance and tenants' welfare and safety – an experience making tenants acutely aware of their own powerlessness. Many tenants spoke of feeling demeaned and stigmatised simply for where they live though many spoke too of pride in their homes and of being well treated by their landlords.

The commission therefore wanted to tackle the reasons why social housing is not working as it has done in the past. It tackled three key areas: the need for and supply of social housing; regulation to enable tenant safety; and issues of tenant participation to challenge the feeling of powerlessness.

The key factor that has had most impact on social housing has been residualisation, the process whereby through scarcity of housing provision, properties that are available are prioritised for those in greatest need. In contrast to earlier intentions of creating mixed communities, social housing has become, in many instances, the housing of last resort. The consequence of this shift has been a much higher concentration of tenants with (often) significant problems such as poor mental health, weak support structures, and substance abuse. This has in turn prompted the labelling of 'sink estates' which reinforces poor images of those who live there. The impact of residualisation is indisputable. The solution is to increase capacity: to build or renovate more homes for use. This is not confined to social housing, for the condition of the PRS has a direct bearing. Indeed, the initial Victorian impetus for much social housing was the inability of the PRS to provide affordable accommodation for a local population, and in many parts of England today this is also the case. Scarcity of housing pushes up asset prices and rental values and makes it harder for local authorities to require developers to ensure much social housing provision.[11]

Social housing providers in urban areas with high land values are in an unenviable position. Gentrification has taken place in many parts of London, with many large estates sold by local authorities and demolished, tenants being relocated to distant areas, or even other cities.[12] Social housing providers there can be faced with the dilemma of maintaining old, costly buildings, or alternatively capitalising on the asset through sale and in its place purchasing newer, more easily maintained properties – but in less popular, distant locations. Tenants may thus experience a process of gentrification even from local housing associations. They may also prefer to stay in overcrowded accommodation – due to the high value they place on remaining in the local community, with its established network of relationships, schooling and access to work – rather than apply for rehousing in better but less conveniently located areas. To some this may sound little different from choices made by owner-occupiers or those who rent privately, but there is an important difference: those in social housing have far less choice in where they live, and often the net value to social housing tenants is higher, because their need of local support systems may be greater (eg, peer support, childminding) than those on higher incomes in the same neighbourhood.

Within the PRS, many tenants fear the threat of eviction if they complain. Increasingly they cannot afford to save for a deposit or mortgage, and remain trapped in the sector. As the population ages, there will be greater need for modifications to properties which private landlords may be reluctant to comply with, thus increasing the scarcity of appropriate housing for elderly people.

The Shelter Commission's recommendations included a call to build more social housing: 3.1m over a 20-year period.[13] The sums to fund this are eye-watering, but comparable to other large infrastructure projects: £10.7bn per year, though when offset by Housing Benefit savings, direct and indirect benefits the figure is much reduced, and in less than 40 years would pay for itself.[14] A new regulator covering both social and private renting is required to set and enforce standards, and tenants' voices need to be heard by landlords and at every tier of government.

Theological reflections

The theological question is: what is the Christian vision of how human beings should live life 'in all its fullness' and what role does social housing play in helping to deliver this?

In considering fullness of life, we need to think not merely of individuals or households in isolation but of the kind of *communities* housing creates. Owner-occupier areas tend to promote people with similar interests, backgrounds and income levels. By contrast, social housing can enhance mixed developments, particularly in inner city areas otherwise inaccessible to all but the most wealthy. We need always to consider the kind of social life that is encouraged or impaired by the nature of one's accommodation.

Let us consider three key themes: how a sense of *home* enables human fulfilment, how it fosters *community*, and the attendant issues of *powerlessness and agency*.

Jesus asserted the importance of having one's own *home*: he condemned those who exploited others' vulnerabilities, citing the 'devouring of widow's houses' (Luke 20: 45 – 47), echoing the prophet Micah (Micah 2:2). He spoke of the promises of God to faithful disciples in terms of a many-roomed divine dwelling, in which there is space for all. Such a sense of one's own space – unconfined, unrestricted and secure – affords the physical and emotional room for one to grow, develop, and fulfil one's potential. Housing and shelter are vital aspects for human well-being, but the key issue is the capacity to make a home. Elements of this include a sense of security, stability, physical and emotional privacy, and the ability to foster a sense of personal or family identity. A home is far more than accommodation; residing in a barracks, hospital ward, prison cell or hotel does not provide these goods, despite the security and welfare each provide. A good home environment is consonant with the Scriptural vision of the blessed life, in which each person shall dwell under 'his' own vine and fig-tree undisturbed (Micah 4:4) secure and free from intrusion or molestation.

Homes are found within *community*. Residents are unlikely to invest time and labour in their communities if they do not have a sense of belonging, for instance through the fear they may have to leave at short notice. At its best, social housing promotes a sense of community and neighbourhood - and Shelter commissioners heard numerous instances of this. Secure residents spoke of pride in the way neighbours decorated communal areas with flowers and garden plants in the knowledge that this was not a wasted effort.

Social housing is a public good, and for both economic and social reasons. Without social housing, many people on lower incomes could not afford to live in the inner cities, or places where they can commute to work easily. Longer and more expensive travel would make it harder for many businesses to find the staff they need, and there would be wage inflationary pressures on those they do employ, with consequent implications for the wider economy. Social housing also helps to provide social diversification and to build stronger, more resilient communities. This may sound strange to those whose image of social housing is large, often prefabricated estates on the edges of cities. Much social housing is in fact in mixed areas, partly through the introduction of Right to Buy in 1981 (when council housing stock was sold at discounted prices to tenants), but also through newer smaller-scale developments. In an area such as North Kensington, multi-million pound house owners live immediately adjacent to neighbours in social housing, and many expensive houses in the area remain seldom used. The contrast is stark, but not so stark if it were comprised of physically separated dwellings, such as in gated communities.

A disturbing finding the Shelter commission observed was the high level of public stigma social housing residents feel, simply because of the kind of housing they live in.[15] This was witnessed in interactions with landlords too: social housing tenants spoke of their feeling treated as second-class citizens when registering concerns or complaints. It is noteworthy that we have one instance recorded in Scripture where Jesus experienced the stigma attached to his social origins as witnessed by Nathaniel's question, 'Can anything good come from Nazareth?' (John 1:46). Christ's incarnation embraces an identification with the stigmatised, with those whose insights and perspectives are dismissed by those with more influence and power. Commissioners were firmly of the opinion that social housing should be for all who wish it, not just for some, and that factors supporting stigmatisation should be removed. The commission therefore advocated 'tenure-blind' developments where the type of occupancy is not visible from the appearance of the property, in contrast to recent developments in which separate 'poor doors' are designed for social housing tenants in mixed developments. The recent furore over the Lilian Baylis estate in London provides a good illustration of such segregated development: social housing families in a mixed development were prevented from accessing a communal area by a wall erected by the developer.[16] Following widespread condemnation the dividing wall was removed.

Tenants' sense of being marginalised due to their social tenancy is linked with the experience of *powerlessness*. This was revealed in the wake of the Grenfell Tower fire, where local residents spoke of safety concerns going unheeded. At the heart of this matter is the imbalance of power between social tenants and their landlords. Owners and lease-holders can choose to make repairs to their properties; in the PRS, tenants can, at least in the theory of the market, choose to seek alternative accommodation if they are not satisfied. Social tenants, perhaps especially those in some of the larger housing conglomerates, can feel divorced from decision-makers, and unaware of how their complaint (a repair, say) is being processed. Strengthening regulation on social housing on a par with consumer regulation, and enhancing tenant voice can only be positive outcomes.

Social housing tenants have often been treated (unfairly) as the recipients of welfare, and not as persons with *agency* of their own. Measures that improve tenants' own sense of self-worth and dignity are clearly vital aspects of any good housing policy. Listening to tenants requires a clear and robust framework, and a willingness to adapt on the part of social landlords, for it is all too easy to be seduced into thinking that one is listening attentively, but in reality only to that which accords with what is expected or deemed acceptable. At the National Commemoration Service for the victims and survivors of the Grenfell Tower fire, held at St Paul's Cathedral, the Rt Revd Graham Tomlin concluded his sermon with a call for those in authority to find a new way 'to listen and to love'. This requires not a little humility on the part of those with power, and a readiness to consider uncomfortable truths about the ways in which systems can fail those they are designed to serve. Only then will tenant participation be regarded as a valuable contribution and not a token gesture.

Social housing as a common good

Housing policy has been shaped by economic forces, and it is clear that the market plays a vital part in the provision and distribution of varieties of housing from ownership to the private rented sector. However, housing issues cannot be reduced to a discussion on the appropriate distribution of commodities for, as we have seen, at the heart of the issue are those conditions which make for, or impair, human flourishing. Therefore, the rationale for long-term social housing policy goes beyond the economic field alone. Ethical and economic considerations are intertwined here, but as with other public goods, interventions and boundaries are needed to prevent a housing system being skewed towards the wealthy and powerful – with consequences for the whole of society.

During the early period of exile in Babylon all the Israelites there were instructed to build homes, settle down, establish patterns of family life and 'seek the welfare of the city…for in its welfare you will find your welfare' (Jeremiah 29:7). Social housing should be guided similarly, that its increase in size and regulation might benefit not just those in greatest housing need, but society as a whole – today and for future generations.

The Revd Dr Mike Long is Minister of the Notting Hill Methodist Church, London

Notes

1. Building for our future: a vision for social housing. The final report of Shelter's Commission on the future of social housing (2019)
2. Shelter figures as reported in *The Guardian*, June 9, 2018.
3. Shelter's latest calculation is 320,000, see https://www.bbc.co.uk/news/education-46289259
4. John Boughton, *Municipal Dreams* (London: Verso, 2018) p.13.
5. John Boughton, *Municipal Dreams* p.8.
6. John Boughton, *Municipal Dreams* pp.14-15.
7. John Boughton, *Municipal Dreams* p.57.
8. John Boughton, *Municipal Dreams* p.105.
9. Commercial pressures and government policy in recent years have led to a sharp reduction in the number of new affordable homes delivered by many housing associations. Figures from NHG for 2017-18 show that only 41 of 991 their newly available properties offered were for social rent.
10. *Building for our future*, p.49.
11. Known as Section 106 (of the 1990 Town and Country Planning Act), this allows local authorities to require developers to commit a proportion of new homes for affordable housing, but there are exemptions. *Building for the Future*, p.125.
12. Anna Minton, *Big Capital* (London: Penguin, 2017).
13. This figure is arrived at by adding those in most pressing need for housing (homeless, dangerous accommodation, overcrowded, ill health, 1.27m) with younger trapped renters (1.17m) for whom buying a property is quite beyond their means [those who will reach age 30 over the next 20 years, calculated at 19% of this population using data from the Resolution Foundation], and 691,000 older renters who similar will never be able to afford alternative accommodation.
14. *Building for the future*, p. 119.
15. *Building for the future*, p.12
16. Over half of social renters say they are portrayed unfairly. *Building for the future*, pp. 39-40.
17. 'London bans segregated play spaces at all new housing sites'. *The Guardian* 20/7/19.

Book Reviews

Christian Mindfulness: Theology and practice
Peter Tyler
SCM Press 2018, 160pp., £19.99

We all stand on the shoulder of others and acknowledging our indebtedness to the legacy that they have left and this awareness is an important part of our nurture of both realism and gratitude. Peter Tyler played a key part in the development of Christian Spirituality here at Sarum College some years ago. So there were high expectations from this book and certainly they were met in these six carefully crafted chapters. Tyler's learning, research and ability to communicate are all brought to bear on the understanding and practice of mindfulness. He is immersed is a wide range of literature and the book combines depth with accessibility.

Tyler uses his generative knowledge of mediaeval mysticism drawing on appreciation of *St Teresa of Ávila and St John of the Cross*. He tackles the synergy between mindfulness and the practice of prayer within the Christian tradition offering a practical model of the ways in which openness to others from a variety of religious traditions can enable the nurture of confidence in one's own identity. Tyler never loses sight of a wider horizon or a desire to enable and empower his reader to deepen a faith that is informed and integrated. With an eye on practice there are a number of helpful exercises inviting the reader into practice.

Chapter 6 (Living a Mindful Life: the Indian Tradition) is particularly interesting in the way it opens up the life and poetry of Rabindranath Tagore and relating it particularly to faith development especially in midlife (133ff). The task of attentiveness, listening and nurturing the spiritual is core in the multiplicity of ways within which any human life and experience attempts to know the divine. In our over active and consumerist religious culture Tyler offers us a different and very much more compelling vision of discipleship through what might be described as a practical theology of human flourishing.

Finally those who might be wondering why such a book should be reviewed in a journal that has as its focus social ethics should be reassured that throughout these chapters and exercises there is a clear imperative that the practice of mindfulness is inextricably interlinked with Christian social action.

This is an excellent book and might be used in a variety of ways: as a wise complement on a retreat or time of reflection; as an opportunity to renew and deepen prayer in the workplace or in a social context such as a house group or a retreat. The reader will certainly be indebted to Peter Tyler for his skill in the quality reflexivity.

James Woodward, Sarum College

The Bible and Disability: A Commentary

Sarah J. Melcher, Mikeal C. Parsons, Amos Yong, eds.
Baylor University Press, 2017, xi + 498pp., pbk, £35.00

This is the first comprehensive commentary from a disability perspective. Numerous, largely compatible, interpretive approaches are employed, which vary in strength and exegetical strain. Melcher's thorough examination of Genesis could be improved by more reflection upon the wider significance of infertility. Her analysis of Exodus 4 is sounder, and considers the sovereignty of God over health and disability. Stewart highlights tensions in the portrayal of the abilities of the Israelite hero in Deuteronomy. He successfully outlines differences between the role of disability in the P source(s) and the JED sources. Schipper is wary of reading into the text. He notes Joshua does not mention disability, despite chronicling Canaan's conquest. He argues that Judges employs disability only for literary effect. In the books of Samuel, Schipper observes that, at first, only antagonists suffer disabilities. Wynn picks up on the issue of interpretation. She considers how the theology that lies behind the choice of vocabulary in Chronicles has consequences for the disabled. Impairment is again a Divine punishment, and she warns against objectifying people. She concludes that dependency serves as a call to relate to God. Melcher highlights the correlation between longevity and wisdom in Proverbs, and challenges this 'tyranny'. In Ecclesiastes, she argues that impairment is normal, as life is ephemeral. Melcher deems worldly justice unreliable for Job, but that he is proved righteous before God through disability. Koosed recognises that, for Psalms, sin manifests itself in bodies, which marginalises the disabled. She holds that pain extends even to the imperfect acrostic structure of Lamentations, and that bodies in the Song of Songs are alluring only because of their strangeness. In Isaiah, Couey argues that disability is normal: it expresses the breakdown in Divine-human relations. In Jeremiah, Couey notes that the post-exilic restoration is made accessible by God specifically for the disabled (Jeremiah 31). He determines that this is a theological discourse about Divine sovereignty over creation.

In Mark and Matthew's Gospels, Candida Moss identifies three attitudes towards disability though these are not always distinguishable in her exegesis. She highlights how moral and physical rectitude correlate in Matthew, which she considers out-of-date. She warns that healing narratives marginalise disability, labelling the Markan Jesus 'a cathartic scourge' of disabled experience (284). Elsewhere, her interpretation of healing more constructively emphasises the porosity of Jesus's body. In Luke, David Watson observes how Jesus unnecessarily touches a leper whilst healing him (Luke 5.12–16), and offers the convincing explanation that Jesus breaks down barriers of exclusion. The boils of Lazarus (Luke 16.19¬¬–31) are reread as a symptom of society's sinfulness. Watson effectively captures some similarities between Luke and social models of disability, without imposing anachronistic sensibilities. Jaime Clark-Soles argues that impaired people are intrinsically valuable in the Johannine literature, as they were created according to the will of God. She notes the irony in John, such as when a blind man sees Jesus coming but the able-bodied Pharisees do not (John 9). Grappling with how to honour suffering without glorifying it, and how society disables its members Clark-Soles is anxious that Revelation's language of conquering adversity alienates disabled persons, but wary of confusing resignation with endurance. He observes that there are images of new life which do not erase the old.

Arthur Dewey and Anna Miller, argue that the Pauline corpus offers a choice—especially significant for the vulnerable—between breaking down (the way of *sarx*) or building up (the way of *pneuma*) the community of God. They stress powerfully a community based on solidarity with the 'disabled Anointed One' (393), and press the case that the weak manifest salvation. 1 Corinthians 15 problematises this interpretation, but their motives are laudable. Wisely, Dewey and Miller do not speculate as to the infirmities of Paul himself. They note the condemnation of domination in Philippians 2.6–8, but are alarmed that Jesus could be seen as a 'heavenly imperial figure' (408). For Dewey and Miller, this image could endanger non-conformers. They conclude that one must always be conscious of the historical context of Scripture and that, for Paul, Jesus' death reveals how God communicates Godself from within human weakness. Martin Albl uses the limits model of disability and sees endurance, prominent in James, as essential for the disabled and for the Christian; though he warns against its romanticisation. He argues that James believes that all people should be welcomed equally, without distinctions based on social status. Finally, in Hebrews, Albl observes that disability is made prominent through the emphasis on Christ's choice to be marginalised.

Generally, *The Bible and Disability: A Commentary* is commendable, despite a few shortcomings. One is the tendency of some authors to over-read the silence of the text. Another is that, in some places, the hermeneutical methods employed could be more clearly articulated. Nevertheless, none of the shortcomings detract too much from the valuable contribution that this highlighting often-neglected narratives, it breaks valuable new ground.

David Mark Dunning, Dublin City University

Sabbath Rest as Vocation; Aging Toward Death
Autumn Alcott Ridenour
T&T Clark, 2018, x + 261pp., hbk, £76.50

Given that Christian theology and belief stem from a narrative of death and resurrection, the focus on a Christological theology of life and resurrection often forsakes a theology of death. Ridenour seeks to address this imbalance by formulating a theology of aging and death utilising Augustine and Barth to construct the meaning of Sabbath rest and participation therein as the process of aging and death.

Ridenour begins by outlining the problematic nature of society's over-valuing of life as seen through various media portrayals of the 'youthful' flawless body; experienced through transhumanism where aging is seen as a disease for which a cure must be found; and finally witnessed within contemporary medical praxis where the denial of death is routinely exercised. All of these examples signify a culture

Book Reviews

in which life is seen as pre-eminent whilst aging (which ultimately leads to death) and death are to be feared, avoided, and denied. The implications of this cultural consensus for medical ethics are stark and it is within this context that Ridenour seeks to challenge this supposedly 'normative' approach to aging and death. Instead she seeks to create a theology in which aging, and death can be seen as part of the flourishing of human existance and relationship to God.

From this introduction the reader is taken on a journey through, first, Augustine's theory and theology of ageing and death in which we become aware of the significant relationship between the body and soul, both assumed and actual. Augustine's complex relationship to the body is explored by Ridenour but never resolved, rather she opens up the Augustinian body-soul dichotomy, concluding that aging individuals are a sign of the sabbath rest and that for Augustine, rest is the end and aim of human existence. We then turn to a Barthian approach to aging and death and are again reminded of the significance of the body-soul relationship as we are taken through the vastness and depth of Barth's theology as it relates to aging and death. The following three chapters take the reader in the direction of participation through Christology as a way of negotiating a theology of aging and death. The final chapter specifically explores Augustinian virtue and Barthian vocation as a way into such Christological participation as transformative and positively enhancing.

Ridenour attempts in this book to offer value to aging and dying bodies. In terms of developing a theology of aging and death I found the dialogue partners of Augustine and Barth to be somewhat limiting in an area which has the potential to be rich in a breadth of theological conversation. Ridenour establishes that life is not the ultimate good, neither is death the ultimate evil. She offers meaning to aging through the theology of Augustine and Barth and finally she points towards the eschatological hope of sabbath rest. For anyone working with those who are aging or approaching death, for anyone engaged in body theology or medical ethics this book offers a particular (and possibly limiting) lens on the potential of a theology of aging and death as it relates to sabbath rest.

Charity Hamilton, Middlesbrough & Eston Circuit

Theology for Changing Times: John Atherton and the Future of Public Theology

Christopher Barker and Elaine Graham, eds.
SCM, 2018, 168pp., pbk, £24.51

This collection of essays edited by Christopher Barker and Elaine Graham reflect on the work and ongoing legacy of John Atherton, a renowned priest, theologian, and scholar of Anglican social ethics who died in 2016. He was also, until his death, a long serving editor of this journal.

A dedicated Lancastrian and Canon Theologian at Manchester Cathedral for twenty years, he was a scholarly heir in the tradition of Archbishop William Temple and profoundly shaped by the tradition which arose from William Temple's association with two architects of the welfare state, Richard Tawney and William Beveridge. Among the first of the world's industrialised cities, Manchester and Salford have a legacy of their own (whether it is the 'Manchester School' or a Manchester story, as argued by Peter Sedgwick in this book) and Atherton rooted his identity as an individual and as a theologian in its particular context. As the home for the William Temple Foundation, of which Atherton was the Secretary and from which seven of this volume's 13 contributors are officially connected, the Manchester/Salford context continues to be a leader in the UK in relation to the intersections between faith, theology, economics, and ethics. Salford was one of the first cities to hold a Poverty Truth Commission in the UK and Manchester is about to start its own, and has a continued strength in faith-based approaches to inequality, marginalisation, fairer economics and social enterprise. Similarly, Atherton's life and work reflects particularities of his context that remained influential throughout his career and in the legacy he leaves behind.

Of course, a volume dedicated to the legacy of a particular scholar is, by nature, uncritical. Instead, this collection of essays focuses on the contributions Atherton made to the area of public theology, reflecting on his contextual foundations and his dedication to autoethnographic style. Additionally, Atherton's approach is refreshingly interdisciplinary, believing that sociology, economics, and psychology must be united and in conversation with theology 'in at least as much as they address the human condition in exploratory and interpretative terms.' (*Challenging Religious Studies: The Wealth, Wellbeing and Inequalities of Nations*, SCM:2014, 194)

The ontology of Atherton's work can be encapsulated with this excerpt from his book *Public Theology for Changing Times*, published in 2000: 'The task is to develop large theologies which connect in critical dialogue with the narratives demanded by global contexts and questions. There can be no retreat from the Christian task of developing public theologies of global proportions.' (viii). Furthermore, in the same work, Atherton highlights his commitment to interdisciplinarity by calling on theology to engage with 'histories of urbanization and industrialisation and their transformation as global processes... great global challenges, from environment to marginalization... developing a familiarity with a variety of disciplines from economics and politics to history and literature [that] is an unfamiliar world to many in churches and theological departments.' (1-2). This certainly reflects this reviewer's own experiences as well.

Throughout these essays, Atherton is portrayed as an advocate for social action based in deep faith and a keen understanding of the historical, economic, political, and sociological forces at play. He emphasised God's presence in the world, who resides among us and takes flesh in our 'practices of solidarity, interdependence, human dignity and "the ways of justice and of peace."' (*Faith in the Nation: A Christian Vision for Britain*, SPCK: 1988, 31)

The contributors to this volume are varied in scope and focus. Most helpfully for this reviewer who was not familiar with Atherton's legacy, Hilary Russell provides a detailed overview of the variety found in Atherton's work and reiterates his emphasis on grassroots issues. Russell helpfully applies this by considering Atherton's advocacy for a 'Christianity fit for purpose', which is one that prioritises and influences and promotes positive well-being, making positive contributions to measurable indicators in tools such as the Social Development Index (Morris, 2011), the Index of Sustainable Economic Welfare (Daly & Cobb, 1990), and the Belonging, Becoming, and Participation Index (Baker, 2013). Similarly, Ann Ruddick focuses on Atherton's commitment to 'missional pastoral care,' based in a commitment to be a 'within and alongside local communities' and working toward a more holistic vision of well-being. Malcolm Brown focuses on Atherton's legacy of mission in a context of industrialisation. As previously mentioned, Peter Sedgwick considers the idea of a Manchester School versus a much larger Manchester story, and identifies Atherton's commitment to 'serious engagement with non-theological sources,' along with 'a stubborn refusal to dodge the hard questions... and a prioritisation of human wellbeing and flourishing' as factors of his work and legacy that are 'quintessentially "Athertonian".' Maria Power's chapter takes a different turn from the rest by taking on Atherton's commitment and rootedness to Anglican social ethics and applies the same approach to her own context of Northern Ireland and Roman Catholic social teaching.

Overall, for anyone interested in wider conversations related to the roots and development of public theology in the UK, this volume is helpful in distilling Atherton's corpus of work. As a non-Anglican and therefore relatively unexposed to Atherton, I very much appreciated reading this volume and am dedicated to giving more focused attention to his work. Atherton's emphasis on connecting theology with real life as told by these contributors is not necessarily new, but given our increasing interconnectedness through global mobility and access to information, the call for theology to be in conversation with these 'global contexts and questions' seems all the more important.

Jayme R. Reaves, Sarum College

Reinhold Niebuhr in the 1960s: Christian Realism for a Secular Age
Ronald H. Stone
Fortress Press, 2019, xii + 206pp., pbk, $34.00.

The last two decades saw Reinhold Niebuhr's reputation entering something of an eclipse, with critiques coming from at least two different directions. The popularity of Stanley Hauerwas' ecclesiologically rooted moral theology, with its Barthian undertones saw Niebuhr's *Christian Realism* offering a compromised Christology, tarnished by too close an encounter with secular influences and reasoning. Making a pincer movement from a very different direction, is the Thomist based moral critique of John Milbank and his *Radical Orthodox* followers. More recently, however, Niebuhrians have made counter attacks, and Reinhold Niebuhr has moved back on to the main stage of moral theology in the realms of both social and political ethics.

Ronald Stone was a pupil and then, later, a friend of Niebuhr, notably in the last two decades of his life. In this book, Stone offers an episodic picture of Niebuhr's work in the 1960s. The fifteen short chapters begin with an introduction, which sets the scene with

Book Reviews

an excellent, albeit brief intellectual biography. Noting the early influence of William James and his philosophical pragmatism, Stone sets Niebuhr in context - with his German Protestant emigre father as the first key influence. He traces Niebuhr's early development, his distancing of himself from Barth, and his greater enthusiasm for the work of Emil Brunner. Effectively, Stone's account continues as an intellectual and political biography, tracing his reaction and response to events, trends and personalities in the final two decades of his life: Niebuhr died in 1971 and had lived with poor health from the 1950s onwards. During these decades, Niebuhr continued to offer a lively critique and direct political comment in what he liked to refer to as a 'secular age'.

There is a recurring series of themes including the nuclear threat, the persistence of racist policies in some states of the USA, concern for the environment and the enduring issue of poverty in his own nation. One of the key organs through which Niebuhr expressed his views was the journal *Christianity and Crisis*, which he had founded and indeed edited, for almost three decades. He continued to publish monographs up until about two years before his death, although the later volumes were largely collections of occasional essays or seminar papers. Niebuhr continued to respond to the changing political situation. He was only moderately enthusiastic about the nomination of John Kennedy as president, and highly critical of the 'Bay of Pigs' fiasco, and the attempted (and bungled) invasions of Castro's Cuba. Later, however, he admired Kennedy's courage and resolve over the Cuban missile crisis.

Stone offers a subtle account of Niebuhr's response to Lyndon Johnson's presidency. He much admired Johnson's impressive social reforms, which included his bringing to a head the abolition of racist laws in the south; Johnson's own Texan background (more unusual for a Democrat) gave him further credence here. His administration did indeed include a variety of Niebuhrians within its number. Niebuhr, however, became increasingly critical of Johnson's handling of the war in Vietnam and, later, of Nixon's record there and of his duplicity. Using classical *Just War* categories, Niebuhr was clear that the action taken was quite disproportionate to the aim; he was also clear that there was 'no reasonable chance of success', in the USA's pursuit of the war. Niebuhr was well aware of Kennedy's responsibility for initially entering the conflict. There were, however, areas where Niebuhr could be surprisingly uncritical: for example, he supported Israel strongly in being the first aggressor in the Six Day War with Egypt and her allies. Nonetheless, elsewhere he was a realist about the US and its illusion of its being a non-imperialist power.

Stone's own friendship with Niebuhr surfaces frequently and, especially, towards the end of his life. They took regular walks together and the accompanying conversation, as they made their way up and down Riverside Drive, on the Upper West Side of Manhattan, allowed Niebuhr to continue to reflect on politics, morals and faith. Stone indicates how important, at different points, Niebuhr's engagement and friendship with Paul Tillich was. Similarly this was true of his converse with Hans J. Morgenthau, the European Jewish political philosopher. This helped hone Niebuhr's ever developing pattern of *Christian Realism*.

This is a most useful book inasmuch as it is unique in describing Niebuhr's late thought and his contribution to both Christian ethics and political life. It also notes the important contribution of Ursula Niebuhr engaging with the same topics in debate with her husband. Perhaps the only criticism of Stone's account is an over-reliance on a chronological analysis, without standing back to review the continuing developing of Niebuhr's thought throughout the final twenty years of his life.

Stephen Platten, Berwick

CHEQUE OR CREDIT CARD		DIRECT DEBIT
Individual rate UK:	☐ £22	☐ £20
Institutional rate UK:	☐ £30	☐ £28
International rate:	☐ £40	☐ £35
Individual copy	☐ £7	

Crucible

Please complete section 1. Cheque **or** 2. Credit/Debit card **or** 3. Direct debit
(the name and address you give must match the information on your credit/Debit card/bank statement.)

YOUR DETAILS (Please complete)

Title .... Christian name .... Surname ....

Address: ....

....

....

Postcode .... Daytime telephone no ....

Email: ....

- I enclose a cheque for the total amount of £..............
  payable to Hymns Ancient and Modern Ltd.
- To pay by credit/debit card please visit www.crucible.hymnsam.co.uk/subscriptions or contact us on 01603 785911

HYMNS Ancient & Modern

Please fill in the whole form using a ball point pen and send to:
Hymns Ancient & Modern Ltd.

Instruction to your bank or building society to pay by Direct Debit

DIRECT Debit

Name and full postal address of your bank or building society

To: The Manager   Bank/building society

Address

Postcode

Name(s) of account holder(s)

Bank/building society account number

Branch sort code

Service user number

| 2 | 4 | 3 | 2 | 3 | 3 |

Reference

| | | | | | | | | | | | | | | | | | |

Instruction to your bank or building society
Please pay Hymns Ancient & Modern Ltd Direct Debits from the account detailed in this Instruction subject to the safeguards assured by the Direct Debit Guarantee. I understand that this Instruction may remain with Hymns Ancient & Modern Ltd and, if so, details will be passed electronically to my bank/building society.

Hymns Ancient & Modern Ltd, 13a Hellesdon Park Road, Norwich NR6 5DR

Signature(s)

Banks and building societies may not accept Direct Debit Instructions for some types of account.

This Guarantee should be detached and retained by the payer.

The Direct Debit Guarantee

DIRECT Debit

- This Guarantee is offered by all banks and building societies that accept instructions to pay Direct Debits.
- If there are any changes to the amount, date or frequency of your Direct Debit Hymns Ancient & Modern Ltd will notify you 10 working days in advance of your account being debited or as otherwise agreed. If you request Hymns Ancient & Modern Ltd to collect payment, confirmation of the amount and date will be given to you at the time of the request
- If an error is made in the payment of your Direct Debit, by Hymns Ancient & Modern Ltd or your bank or building society, you are entitled to a full and immediate refund of the amount paid from your bank or building society
  - If you receive a refund you are not entitled to, you must pay it back when Hymns Ancient & Modern Ltd asks you to
- You can cancel a Direct Debit at any time by simply contacting your bank or building society. Written confirmation may be required. Please also notify us

www.ingramcontent.com/pod-product-compliance
Ingram Content Group UK Ltd.
Pitfield, Milton Keynes, MK11 3LW, UK
UKHW030903050526
12271UKWH00017B/176